SYNCHRONISED SWIMMING

Helen Elkington and Jane Chamberlain

SYNCHRONISED SWIMMING

Foreword by Caroline Holmyard

DAVID & CHARLES

In loving memory of Jim Sullivan

Cox and Holland, 1977 European Championships (*Swimming Times*)

British Library Cataloguing in Publication Data

Elkington, Helen
   Synchronised swimming.
   1. Synchronised swimming
   I. Title   II. Chamberlain, Jane
   797.2'1   GU837

   ISBN 0-7153-8726-X

Text and photographs © Helen Elkington and Jane Chamberlain 1986
Diagrams © Helen Elkington and David & Charles 1986

Typeset by Typesetters (Birmingham) Ltd
Smethwick, West Midlands
and printed in Great Britain
by Butler & Tanner Limited, Frome and London
for David & Charles Publishers plc
Brunel House   Newton Abbot   Devon

Published in the United States of America
by David & Charles Inc
North Pomfret   Vermont 05053   USA

Contents

Carolyn Wilson & Caroline Holmyard (*Sporting Pictures UK*)

Foreword

Synchronised swimming is a relatively new sport, having its Olympic debut at the 1984 Los Angeles Summer Games. It is a discipline which is still developing, but this book offers a clear insight to the many skills and techniques required. Valuable advice is not only given to those setting up a group, but also to those in established clubs.

Although synchronised swimming is a specialist sport, the authors show that it can be enjoyed at many levels, giving a unique opportunity to combine movement, water and music – in groups or as individuals.

Good luck and have fun!

Caroline Holmyard
1984 Olympic Soloist

Carolyn Wilson (*The Swimming Times*)

Introduction

Synchronised swimming is a sport that links great technical skill with creativity and artistry and produces something which is aesthetically pleasing to watch but very difficult to perform. It can perhaps best be compared with ice-skating, where set figures are performed as one part of a competition and then combined with linking movements to form a free programme. In synchronised swimming there are also set figures, which are given a tariff (1.1 to 2.3) according to the degree of difficulty. These are linked together with synchronised swimming strokes and sculling to create routines to music. There are many set figures but it is also possible for swimmers to create their own variations, which are known as 'hybrids'. Routines may be swum by one swimmer (solo), two swimmers (duet), or by four or more swimmers (team).

A good level of general swimming is essential for the synchronised swimmer – proficiency in all four strokes is desirable – as is an ability to 'count' in music and to keep in time with rhythm.

Synchronised swimming strokes are adapted from normal strokes. Mainly front crawl, back crawl and breaststroke are used, with differences in style: the head is up so that the swimmer can see and hear; the arms create the aesthetic effect; and the leg kick is low so that it doesn't distract attention from the arms.

The technique of sculling, vital for synchronised swimming, uses a hand and arm action to support and propel the body. Sculling is particularly important in figures when the swimmer is inverted, keeping the body up while the legs create the 'effect' above the water. There are many sculls and these are discussed in depth in Chapter 3.

Children can be introduced to synchronised swimming skills very early on. They enjoy sculling to music or a drum beat, which helps them to count and keep in time, and benefit from learning simple figures – tub, oyster, somersault back tuck. These can be taught as elementary watermanship activities in the primary school swimming programme, and partnered or group routines can be developed.

At secondary level, synchronised swimming can be a very challenging alternative for those who want more than normal swimming. It is also a natural progression for those who are very able swimmers but do not want to go into competitive speed swimming. Many schools now include

Five Nations Competition, Crystal Palace 1984 (*The Swimming Times*)

synchronised swimming in their curriculum, and the English Schools Championships are held annually.

Disabled swimmers find sculling a very good way of propelling themselves when normal swimming strokes are inappropriate; and both children and adults who are disabled enjoy the challenge of sculling to music and performing simple figures. Simple routines can be created which provide stimulus and give a great degree of satisfaction.

Age is no barrier to the sport; adult classes can be most rewarding. A club in Bedford boasts an age range of eighteen to sixty-seven! The benefits of this type of group are many. It is definitely a social gathering – new friends are made and much enjoyment is had. Fitness is also a primary feature. Swimmers should swim regularly to enable them to cope with the demands of synchronised swimming, and should be confident both above and under water (see Chapter 7). Swimming to suitable music is fun and relaxing and gives room for creativity. Routines can be swum which are challenging and satisfying. Clubs also cater for those swimmers who wish to aim high in the sport, perhaps entering competitions at regional, national or international level. In 1984 synchronised swimming was included for the first time in the Olympic Games in Los Angeles.

It is a marvellous sport and has so much to offer, whatever the need of its participants.

1 General Principles

POOL SUITABILITY

The ideal pool for synchronised swimming should be at least 12m (40ft) in length and in width. The depth of the water is also very important. For competition and also for figure work the depth needs to be 3m (10ft); for routines, the depth has to be 2m (6ft).

It is inevitable that many school and club pools may not always have ideal dimensions and this should be taken into account when planning activities. If the pool is shallow, then surface figures such as somersault front/back tucks, marlin, tub, single and double ballet legs, can be performed safely, as can formation swimming and floating activities.

SAFETY AND HYGIENE

At all synchronised swimming sessions both teacher and pupils must observe strict standards of safety and hygiene. It is essential that everyone is familiar with the following rules:

1 No swimmer should enter the pool until permission is given.
2 Swimmers should be aware of pool dimensions, especially depth.
3 There must be *no running* on the poolside.
4 Pushing in must be strictly forbidden.
5 Swimmers must know exactly what to do in an emergency. A warning whistle can be used but everyone must know how to respond to the signal.
6 Everyone should know where to obtain first-aid equipment.
7 Safety equipment – poles, life-belts and ropes – should be strategically placed and the swimmers made familiar with their use.
8 Teachers and coaches must have sound working knowledge of the methods of resuscitation, especially the expired air method. They should also be competent swimmers themselves and be able to rescue any pupil who gets into difficulty.
9 No swimmer should enter the pool immediately after a heavy meal.
10 Swimmers should not chew gum during a water session.
11 No one should swim with any foot or skin infection.
12 No one should swim with a cold or an ear infection.
13 No outdoor shoes should be worn on the poolside.

14 Showers and toilets should be used before a swimmer enters the pool.

15 All jewellery should be removed before a swimmer enters the pool.

16 Swimmers with long hair should wear swimming hats.

17 Swimming costumes should be thoroughly rinsed and wrung out after use.

EQUIPMENT

The correct equipment can make a synchronised swimming session 'come to life', but careful consideration should be given before any purchases are made.

The most important item is the cassette player. This should give good quality of sound and be battery-operated to avoid the possible dangers of electrical equipment on the poolside.

A selection of cassettes should be purchased. Choose instrumental music which is suited to the age and ability of the pupils and has a clearly defined beat. Certain pieces of music lend themselves to a particular stroke and lively tunes help to get a session going. An underwater speaker is also important. This enables the swimmers to hear the music clearly whilst they are submerged, which is essential in routine work when swimmers must keep in time with the rhythm.

A drum or tambour can also provide accompaniment. It should have a plastic face as parchment does not stand up too well to the damp atmosphere.

One of the most useful teaching aids is a 'plastic man' (artists would call this a lay figure). This is about a foot long and is made from hard plastic, jointed so that it can be manipulated to show body positions. It is much easier for a swimmer to see what is required instead of listening to a long technical explanation.

Beginners who find it difficult to keep their feet at the water surface while sculling benefit from having an armband around each ankle – a very simple but effective piece of equipment (though its use must be carefully supervised by a teacher). Poles are also useful to manipulate a swimmer into a required body position. Obviously a degree of care should be used by the operator! Ropes should be available to divide the pool into sections for mixed ability use. They are also used for dividing the pool into lanes for general fitness training.

TEACHER/PUPIL RELATIONSHIP

The teacher of synchronised swimming has to work in an extremely difficult environment, but she must make every effort to promote a happy relationship with her pupils. (NB We use 'she' because girls predominate in this sport, though it could of course be 'he'.)

First impressions are very important. She should wear appropriate clothing, eg a tracksuit and poolside shoes – never outdoor shoes – when giving instructions. Her manner should be pleasant and enthusiastic, with an easy sense of humour, and she should offer plenty of constructive advice.

A teacher must ensure that pupils can see her for the purpose of effective demonstration and that she can see them clearly for reasons of safety. Her voice plays a vital part: it can be an inspiration or it can be a bore. Enunciation, speed of delivery, volume and expression are all important and need to be varied according to the situation. The further the teacher is from a pupil, the louder and more slowly she will need to speak. A good motto is 'Don't talk too much'. Too much talk means too little swimming! Instructions should be short and to the point and the teacher should encourage the pupils to think by asking questions and making appropriate use of the answers.

DEMONSTRATIONS

Demonstrations are essential to any synchronised swimming session. They can be given by the teacher or by an able pupil to accompany a verbal description. Demonstrations must be technically accurate and must be clearly visible to the pupils in the water. The positioning of the teacher on the poolside is a very important factor to consider.

The watching class should not be looking directly into the sun. The teacher should let the pupils see the demonstration from different angles, ie side on, head on, depending on what points she wants to emphasise. For example, a demonstration of standard scull emphasising 'fingertips up' would be best seen side on, whereas a demonstration of standard scull emphasising the figure-of-eight movement of the hands and the straight elbows would be best viewed head on.

The teacher should adopt as accurate a body position as possible so that the pupils can translate her movements to their situation in the water. If, for instance, she is demonstrating canoe travel, a prone position should be adopted by balancing on one leg and leaning forward with the other leg stretched out behind. Where a supine position is needed, the teacher could make use of a bench or a chair on the poolside, for instance when demonstrating bent-arm back crawl.

2 Strokes

Synchronised swimming strokes are much more difficult than the normal swimming strokes. Their function is to cover the pool area, creating interesting patterns, and to serve as transitions from figure to figure. They should be pleasing to watch and enable swimmers to work with one another and to an accompaniment. Beauty, and not speed, is the all-important feature. Adaptations must be made to normal strokes and some of these are easier to learn than others. It is suggested that the breaststroke and back crawl are introduced *before* the front crawl. A good teacher must observe the pupils to decide how best to guide them. Each stroke should be analysed in terms of body position, leg action and so on, as detailed below, and with practice any weaknesses can be recognised.

ANALYSIS OF STROKES
Body Position
The body is inclined with the hips well under water. The head is raised and held high and steady, the eyes looking directly forwards. The facial expression should be cheerful but not fixed.

Leg Action
The inclined-body position increases resistance and necessitates an efficient leg kick. The leg kick propels the body, balances it and keeps it up. In front and back crawl the flutter-type kick is deeper than usual and the legs should not break the water surface as this would detract from the stroke gestures being made by the arms. The breaststroke kick should be symmetrical. A side kick is often used too.

Arm Action
The arm action is used mainly for expression, maintaining height, balancing the body and a certain amount of propulsion. The arm gestures should be attractive and, whether recovering over or in the water, create pleasing patterns. The arm action can portray the mood of the accompaniment by variations in speed and patternwork.

In an alternating stroke the arm recovering over the water is used for visual effect whereas the arm in the water sculls hard to balance the body and to keep it up.

14

Breathing

Breathing is obviously necessary! It should be regular, quiet and controlled. Coughing and spluttering will spoil the stroke.

Timing

The stroke rhythm will vary according to the music used and the mood of the sequence. The rhythm should give the impression of fluency and be attractive to the spectator.

EGG-BEATER KICK

The egg-beater kick is frequently used instead of a front-crawl flutter kick. It exerts an alternate downward pressure which is continuous, therefore the body travels smoothly and with stability, avoiding a bobbing movement. Using this kick it is possible to gain height or easily change direction during travel if desired.

The *body* is in a vertical position similar to the treading water position for life saving/survival. The *legs* are bent so that the thighs are at an angle of 90 degrees to the trunk. The knees are wider than hip width apart. The *lower* legs are responsible for the alternating cycling movement, with the knees maintaining the same level throughout. The lower left leg circles anti-clockwise and the lower right leg clockwise, or vice versa. It is similar to sitting on a table with the thighs resting on the top and the lower legs moving alternately. To start the kick the left leg is held almost parallel to the

Egg-beater kick from above

Underwater view of the egg-beater kick   Land practice for egg-beater kick

pool bottom with the foot dorsiflexed (bent upwards or flattened) so that it is at 90 degrees to the shin. The right leg then adopts an identical position as the left leg begins to circle. According to the direction of movement, ie clockwise or anti-clockwise, the leg movement will be forwards or backwards and in both cases downwards. Continuous pressure is essential.

The *arms* can be used to support the body. They can be kept *in* the water and a flat scull used or, if desired, raised out of the water to create an aesthetically pleasing gesture. The head is held in a high steady position as if balancing a pint of milk on the top. Facial expression should be cheerful but not fixed, and breathing quiet, regular and under control.

BACK CRAWL

The *head* is raised to see and hear, and should be steady. The *body* is inclined with a diagonal slope to the legs and kept stable.

The *leg kick* is an alternating flutter kick working in the vertical plane. The movement is initiated from the hips, with the legs as straight as possible and swinging rhythmically, passing closely. The upward kick is about a foot below the water surface – the legs and feet should not break the surface. The downward kick is 1ft to 18in from the top of the upward kick.

For the *arm action*, as one arm is recovering over the water, the arm in the water is working hard with a sculling action to facilitate the expressive movements of the overwater arm. The underwater sculling is essential, therefore, for balance, keeping the body up and a certain amount of

16

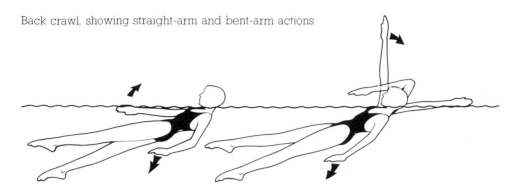

Back crawl, showing straight-arm and bent-arm actions

propulsion. The patterns overwater can vary and are very much affected by musical rhythm, the ability and imagination of the performer and the expression necessary to attract the spectator.

Breathing should be controlled, regular and quiet with a pleasant facial expression.

Timing will vary according to mood and rhythm.

Bent-arm Back Crawl
The arm leaving the water is bent during recovery with a high elbow shown (see also p109). The arm under water sculls to balance.

Straight-arm Back Crawl
The arm leaving the water is held straight firmly, thumb clearing the water first. As the extended arm reaches the vertical it is rotated so that it enters the water in advance of the head, little finger first. The hand should be firm, fingers together. As the hand clears and enters the water it is like the blade of a knife. The arm under water sculls to balance.

Tap-tap Back Crawl
The right arm, for example, leaving the water is held straight and firmly, thumb clearing the water first. With the hand palm downwards the arm moves across the body and touches the water by the left hip. It then moves to touch the water, hand palm down, by the right hip. The extended arm is now raised, thumb leading the way, over water in recovery. As it reaches the vertical it is rotated so that it enters the water in advance of the head, little finger first.

BREASTSTROKE
The *head* is held high and steady during the orthodox breaststroke. The eyes should be looking forwards and the shoulders square. There is a slope to the hips and the *body* is inclined.

The *leg kick* is symmetrical. The *wedge* kick is low and can be described in two phases – bend and drive. Bend: the knees are bent outwards and the heels kept together with the soles of the feet facing backwards. The legs are in a diamond position at this point with about a 90-degree angle between the trunk and thighs. Drive: the legs start to kick outwards with the soles of the feet pressing against the water; when the legs have extended they are squeezed together into a stretched 'glide' position.

The *whip kick* can also be used but it must be remembered that after every kick there should be a glide position and the hips are still low. This kick requires greater knee and ankle mobility. The whip kick is often described in three phases – bend, turn and drive. Bend: the legs and feet commence from an extended position (close together). The feet are drawn up towards the seat by bending and parting the knees and thighs until they are slightly wider apart than hip width. The angle between the trunk and thigh at this point is never less than 90 degrees. The feet during this phase are soles uppermost, toes pointing backwards, and they part a few inches as they travel towards the seat. They are dorsiflexed with the toes still pointing backwards during the latter part of the bend. Turn: this part of the kick is essential to its success as it enables the inner borders of the lower legs and feet to prepare for the drive back against the water. The feet, still dorsiflexed, are everted (cocked outwards). The soles are still facing uppermost. The inner borders of the feet and lower legs present a useful surface for driving backwards. Drive: the feet, still everted and dorsiflexed, commence the backward drive. The path is backwards and slightly outwards. The swimmer should concentrate on the heels drawing a circular pattern as they travel backwards. The feet and legs should be extended and together on the completion of the drive.

The orthodox *arm action* can be described under three headings – pull, bend and glide. Pull: this is from an extended position with the arms, hands and fingers together, and palms downwards just under the water surface. The arms are used like paddles. The hands are held firmly, elbows straight. As the pull commences, the hands turn slightly outwards, pulling sideways, backwards and downwards until reaching a point just in front of the shoulders where they should be slightly wider apart than shoulder width. The arms will balance the body in this position. Bend: after the pull the arms are tucked tightly to the sides of the body, elbows by the ribs, hands underneath the chin, palms downwards, like a dog 'begging'. Glide: the arms are extended forwards to a position in front of the body. There should

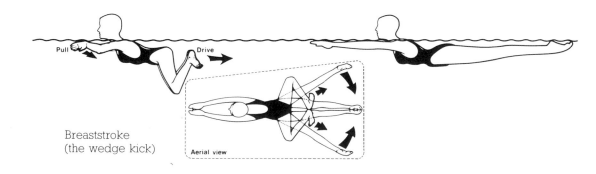

Breaststroke
(the wedge kick)

be a glide before the next pull commences, if the leg kick is effective, to make full use of the leg drive.

Breathing is as follows: preferably exhale or 'blow the hands forward' into the glide position and inhale during the pull phase of the arm action.

Timing will vary according to the stroke variation used. In the orthodox version the arms and legs move together in the glide or extended position. The arms pull and the legs remain extended. As the elbows are tucked to the side and the hands brought under the chin, the legs bend. The feet are turned outwards and drive backwards while the arms extend forwards into the glide position. The position should be held for a short time before the cycle recommences.

In the push stroke (see below) the hands push forwards as the legs kick backwards.

In the side-sweep stroke (see below), as one arm sweeps back the legs kick back; as the elbow bends and the arm extends forward, the legs bend.

Push Stroke

As the arms are extended forwards into the glide position the hands, held firmly, point fingertips upwards and the palms push against the water surface. They create a small splash as they extend forwards.

Side-sweep

The swimmer commences with a small orthodox arm action then, for example, the right hand is turned onto its side, thumb down, palm against the water. The right arm sweeps backwards just at the water surface, making a small splash. When it has completed a full sweep back the elbow bends and the arm is tucked to the side, being brought forwards into a glide position just under the water. During the back sweep of the right arm, the left arm remains extended in a glide position in front of the body. A small orthodox arm action is executed before another side-sweep stroke, this time with the left arm. The eyes of the swimmer should follow the hand of the sweeping arm in this stroke variation.

FRONT CRAWL

(It is recommended that this is introduced after the back crawl and breaststroke.)

The *head* is raised and steady, eyes looking directly forwards. The *body* is inclined with a diagonal slope to the legs and should be stable.

The *leg kick* is an alternating flutter kick working in the vertical plane. The movement is initiated from the hips, the legs should be as straight as possible and swung rhythmically, passing closely. The upward kick is about a foot below the water surface – the legs and feet should not break the surface. The downward kick is 1ft to 18in from the top of the upward kick. The egg-beater kick (see p15) can also be used with this stroke.

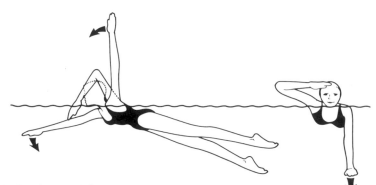

Front crawl, showing straight-arm bent-arm and salute actions

For the *arm action*, as one arm is recovering over the water the arm in the water is working hard with a sculling action to facilitate the expressive movements of the overwater arm. The underwater sculling is essential, therefore, for balance, keeping the body up and a certain amount of propulsion.

Breathing is regular, controlled and quiet. Try to exhale or blow out as *one* arm pulls and as that same arm clears the water, breathe in. Close the mouth before the arm re-enters the water. Repeat.

Timing will vary according to the pattern used.

Bent-arm Front Crawl

The arm leaving the water can be bent and show a high elbow in recovery. The arm under water sculls to balance. Alternatively, the arm leaving the water can be extended thumb upper-most and bent to the high elbow position during recovery. The arm re-enters the water fingertips first.

Front view of bent-arm front crawl. Note balancing effect of underwater arm

Straight-arm Front Crawl

The extended arm leaves the water thumb uppermost. Overwater recovery is made in a semi-circular arc. The body during this variation is more on its side. The arm re-enters the water thumb first.

Salute Front Crawl

The recovery is identical to the bent arm but before re-entering the water the hand is placed at eyebrow level in a salute position, elbow still bent. The arm re-enters the water fingertips first.

DOLPHIN BUTTERFLY STROKE

This stroke is rarely used in synchronised swimming, except by an experienced swimmer and then for only a comparatively short time. It is, however, an excellent stroke in a fitness training programme.

SIDE STROKE

This is a breaststroke-type movement where the swimmer adopts a position on the side. The head can rest on one side and the legs execute a scissor movement. The arms are both in a bent position under the head, hands palms down. The lower arm extends forwards under water and the upper arm, palm pressing against the water, presses backwards to full extension. Both arms return to the bent position again under water. The legs kick in the scissor action as one arm extends forwards and the other presses backwards.

HYBRID STROKES

An imaginative, more experienced swimmer will often move away from the uniform synchronised swimming strokes and make up many variations according to the musical interpretation. A hybrid stroke combines the features of several strokes.

CHANGING STROKES

The swimmer will execute, for example, 8 back crawl strokes and on the 8th stroke roll onto the front and continue front crawl for 8 strokes, then change into breaststroke. The changes should be *smooth* and require a great deal of practice.

PRACTICE FOR SYNCHRONISED SWIMMING STROKES

Regular practice of the following exercises will help swimmers to perform the strokes smoothly and with control, and accustom them to working in time to music and with partners (see also Chapter 6). The teacher should stress one teaching point, rather than several, at a time. (TP=teaching points.)

Breaststroke

1 Legs only, breaststroke kick, holding a float.
Pupils widthways across the pool.
TP Arms extended holding the top end of the float. Head high and steady, chin on the water surface. Breaststroke kick with a glide. Control breathing.
2 Legs only, breaststroke kick. Arms stretched and thumbs locked.
Pupils widthways across the pool.
TP As for 1.
3 Full-stroke breaststroke with a glide.
Pupils widthways across the pool.
TP Steady, high head. Chin on the water surface. Glide. Control breathing.

BACK CRAWL

1 Legs only. Holding a float to chest.

Pupils widthways across the pool.

TP Head raised, enabling the swimmer to see and hear. Control breathing. Leg kick low in the water – no splash at surface. Legs must work hard to maintain body position, balance and propulsion.

2 Legs only, hands on thighs.

Pupils widthways across the pool.

TP As for 1.

3 Legs only, hands raised a few inches out of the water.

Pupils widthways across the pool.

TP As for 1.

4 Back crawl, arms included.

Pupils widthways across the pool.

TP Low kick as for legs only. Head high. Arms create pattern and effect. Lift one arm out of the water elbow first, high and bent. Extend the arm for re-entry into the water. The other arm in the water sculls to balance. The strokes should be graceful, controlled and flowing. Movements are phrased to suit a rhythm as well as other swimmers.

Breaststroke and Back Crawl

1 To a drum beat.

Pupils widthways across the pool. Individually and then with partner(s). Progress to swimming in ranks, lengthways.

TP Breaststroke: stretch arms forward into glide on heavy drum beat and pull on 2 light drum beats. Backcrawl: lift right arm out of the water on heavy beat and 2 light beats. Arm then re-enters the water and pulls to side. Repeat with the left arm.

Front Crawl

1 Legs only. Thumbs locked, arms stretched in advance of the head.

Pupils widthways across the pool.

TP Head raised. Chin on the water. The head must be steady. Low kick with no splash.

2 Legs only. Arms held extended behind the shoulders clear of the water by a few inches in a wing-like effect.

Pupils widthways across the pool.

TP As for 1.

3 Full stroke.

Pupils widthways across the pool.

TP Head raised and steady with the chin on the water. Leg kick is low in the water. One arm lifts out of the water with the elbow bent and high. The arm which is in the water sculls to balance the recovery arm.

4 Full stroke to a drum beat.

Pupils widthways across the pool, individually at first and then with partner(s).

TP Lift right arm out of the water on a heavy beat. On 2 light beats the arm re-enters the water and scull pulls to the hip. Repeat with the left arm.

Front and Back Crawl

1 Legs only, to a drum beat. Change from one kick to another on a heavy beat.

Pupils widthways across the pool.

TP Low leg kick, smooth change from back to front, eg on back legs only; 16 light beats, then heavy beat, tuck up and onto front legs only; 16 light beats.

Back Crawl, Front Crawl and Breaststroke

1 To music. Changing from one stroke to another and keeping the flow going.

Pupils widthways across the pool: (a) individually; (b) with one or two partners. Then lengthways in ranks.

TP Keep in time with the music and with partners. Swim back crawl for 8 strokes, roll onto the front and proceed with front crawl and breaststroke. Work on smooth changes.

Swimmers can work on many more variations for each stroke. These should be first taught and practised without an accompaniment and individually. As swimmers become more able at the variations, add challenges, ie working with partners and to percussion or music.

The egg-beater kick should be practised with the arms in and out of the water. Commencing lengthways, work facing the direction of travel, turn and travel sideways, turn and travel backwards. Repeat. Music can be played and if the arms are used it is fun if the swimmers bring in a clap to the rhythm as they travel. Work for stability and height.

The egg-beater kick can also be practised sitting on a diving board and executing the alternating movement.

BREATH CONTROL

Pupils should appreciate and understand breathing and breath control. It can be very distracting when a swimmer involved in a group activity arrives at the water surface spluttering! It is frequently necessary to control the desire to exhale loudly. Some suggested breathing activities are given below. (TP=teaching point.)

Practice

1 Pupils space out and swim breaststroke widthways or lengthways. They

FORMATION CHANGES

The swimmers should vary their patterns/formation when working with others. Changing formation during stroke training is very worthwhile. Some suggested line patterns are:

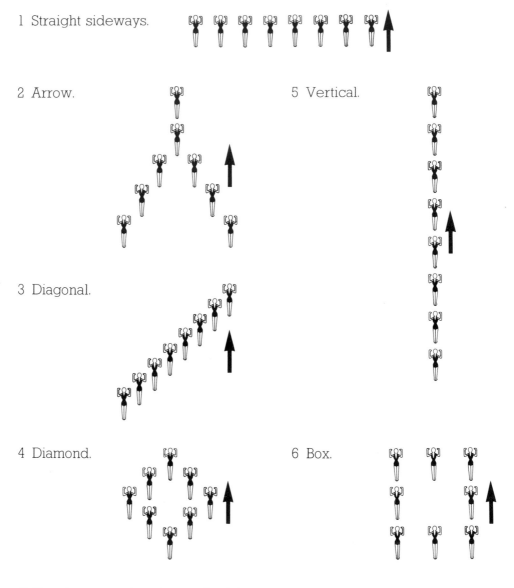

1 Straight sideways.

2 Arrow.

3 Diagonal.

4 Diamond.

5 Vertical.

6 Box.

7 Two breaststrokes forwards; 2 breaststrokes sideways, to the right and forwards; 2 breaststrokes forwards; 2 breaststrokes sideways and to the left and forwards. Repeat.

8 Eight back crawl strokes; on 8th stroke tuck onto front and return with 8 front crawl strokes.

9 Eight back crawl strokes; on 8th stroke roll onto front and carry on in the same direction in front crawl.

surface dive and do several breaststroke cycles under water.

TP Under water exhale gently through the nose and mouth and continue to the surface. On arrival control exhalation.

2 Pupils stand spaced out in the shallow end of the pool and submerge and surface in time to music or a drum beat.

TP Synchronise to the beat and control exhalation. Smile on surfacing. Close mouth before submerging.

3 Lengthwise, swim breaststroke for 4 strokes and on the 5th and 6th counts execute a somersault front tuck (see Chapter 4). Continue with breaststroke.

TP Maintain smoothness of action into compact tucked somersaults and back into strokes again. Keep in time with the rhythm of the music.

SUGGESTED MUSIC FOR PRACTICES

Activity	Music
Alternate flutter kick and change of direction.	'Spuds', Brendan Shine. Cassette: 'My Old Country Home', Play 1c 1017. 'Snowbird', Anne Murray. Cassette: 'Best Friends', TC-IMP.
Egg-beater kick.	'Spuds', Brendan Shine (as above). 'Races of Killadoor', Brendan Shine (as above). 'Pie in the Face' polka (energetic!), James Galway and Henry Mancini. Cassette: 'In the Pink', RCA RK 85315.
Submerging to specific beats.	'Song of the Narobi Trio', Hot Butter. Cassette: Popcorn, Hallmark SHM 852.
Submerging, then rising with smile.	'On Top of Old Smokey', Mrs Mills. Cassette: 'Mrs Mills Party', World Records TC-SH 2600764.
Breaststroke.	'Roses from the South', James Last. Cassette: 'Roses from the South', Polydor 3151 051. 'Thank You for the Music', Abba. Cassette: 'Thank You for the Music', Epic EPC 40-10043.
Breaststroke and slow back crawl.	'I Just Called to Say I Love You', Stevie Wonder. Cassette: 'Woman in Red', Motown ZK 72285.
Breaststroke and somersault.	'Top of the World', The Carpenters. Cassette: 'Yesterday Once More', EMI TC SING I.
Back crawl.	'Rondo Veneziano', Rondo Veneziano. Cassette: 'The Genius of Venice', ZC RON2.
Back crawl and front crawl.	'Fiesta', Royal Philharmonic Orchestra. Cassette: 'Fiesta' (band 1, side 2), CBS 40-25083.
Variety of strokes.	Various tunes by Bobby Crush. Cassette: 'Singalong Party', Warwick label 5138. Various tunes by Mrs Mills. Cassette: 'Mrs Mills Party', World Records TC-SH 2600764. 'This is My Song', James Last. Cassette: 'Love, This is My Song',

Variety of strokes.

Polydor 3150-235. 'Games That Lovers Play', James Last (as above). 'Super Trouper', Abba. Cassette: 'Super Trouper', Epic label EPC 40-10022. 'Dancin' Banjos', Big Ben Banjo Band. Cassette: EMI TC SH 1078214. 'There's a Kind of Hush', The Carpenters, Cassette: 'Yesterday Once More', EMI TC SING I. 'Sing', The Carpenters (as above). 'Rose of Castlerea', Brendan Shine. Cassette: 'My Old Country Home', Play 1c 1017. 'Bone Shaker', Brendan Shine (as above). 'If You Knew Sousa' Cassette: 'If You Knew Sousa – Hooked on Classics 2', Louis Clark conducting The Royal Philharmonic Orchestra OCE 2173. 'Tales of the Vienna Waltz' (as above).

3 Sculling

Sculling is an arm and hand action used to propel, balance and control the body in figures, strokes and transitions. The same basic figure-of-eight action is used in all sculls, ie the hands describe a figure-of-eight in the water. The position of the arms and hands in relationship to the body will vary according to the swimmers' requirement. Even the simplest figure requires more than one scull to be used and an advanced figure will need several different sculls.

All sculls should be smooth, with continuous force applied in the direction opposite to travel or balance. The speed varies, increasing when a leg is bent or raised out of the water. During a figure the position of the arms will alter if the body changes shape, eg from the inverted-vertical position with both legs together into a bent-knee position (see Chapter 4 for layouts and body positions).

Three main sculls are probably most useful to beginners:

1 Standard, or head first.
2 Reverse, or feet first.
3 Flat, or stationary.

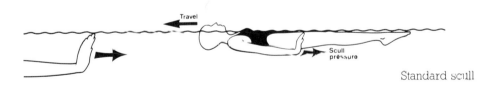

Standard scull

STANDARD SCULL

This is a propelling scull used for travelling head first. The swimmer starts in a back layout with the body extended and the face, hips, knees and toes at the surface. The eyes look up. The arms are held by the sides, with straight elbows. The hands are firm and flat, fingers together with the tips up, just under the hips and close to the body. The wrists are hyper-extended. With a rhythmic movement the hands describe a figure-of-eight, ie as they move outwards the thumbs draw the first half of the 'eight' and as they move inwards the little fingers draw the second half. The pressure of the scull is towards the feet.

REVERSE SCULL

This is a propelling scull used for travelling feet first. The body position is as for the standard scull. The arms are held straight by the sides, with wrists flexed and fingertips pointing to the bottom of the pool. The same figure-of-eight movement is used, as for the standard scull, with the pressure towards the head. Many swimmers try a small breaststroke type of action when learning this scull.

Reverse scull

FLAT SCULL

This is a supporting scull used when the body must be held stationary. The body is in a back layout as for the standard and reverse sculls. The arms are by the sides with straight elbows. The hands are firm and flat, palms down and fingers together. During sculling the arms stay close to the body and the hands move sideways slightly away from the body. The movement is initiated from the shoulders. As the hands move outwards in the figure-of-eight, the little fingers, slightly raised, are leading; the thumbs are then raised to lead on the inward movement. The pressure of the scull is towards the pool bottom.

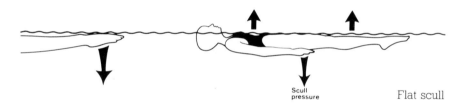

Flat scull

Once pupils have learnt the basic sculls they can progress to other, more advanced sculls. Some of the following require a great deal of practice before they can be accomplished smoothly and easily.

CANOE TRAVEL – STANDARD SCULL

The body is on the front, with the back arched slightly so that the chin and heels are on the water surface. The arms are held straight, by the sides of the body. The wrists are hyper-extended so that the palms face the feet; fingertips point downwards. The body should travel smoothly, head first. The buoyant swimmer will generally place the arms outside body width whereas the non-buoyant swimmer will place the arms just under the hips.

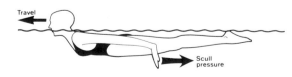

Canoe travel

CANOE (STATIONARY) – FLAT SCULL

The body is in the canoe position. The elbows are usually bent with the hands placed flat, thumb to thumb, fingertips forward, under the bottom rib area. The hands press down and move out, then press down and move in. The swimmer has to work hard to maintain the canoe position. A non-buoyant swimmer often finds it preferable to place the hands by the hips, fingertips pointing out, and, with the thumb knuckles leading the way, to flat scull up and down the side of the trunk. Many swimmers practise this with their feet hooked in the trough at the poolside.

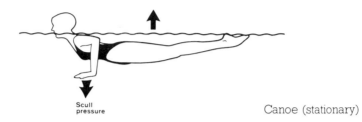

Canoe (stationary)

TORPEDO – STANDARD SCULL

The body is on the back, arms stretched beyond the head. The wrists are hyper-extended and the fingers point towards the pool bottom. The sculling should be smooth, rhythmic and continuous. (I usually say to swimmers 'dust underneath the shelf'.) The arm action is narrow and travel should be feet first.

Torpedo

DOLPHIN (REVERSE TORPEDO) – REVERSE SCULL

The body is on the back, arms stretched beyond the head. The wrists are bent and the hands held firmly ready to 'dust the top of the shelf'. The little fingers are placed in the water and the thumb knuckles are held up. The hands then move at the wrist so that the thumbs are placed in the water and the little fingers are held up. Pressure is to the feet and travel is head first. If the swimmer's feet and legs sink they must be held in place by using the tummy muscles. Under strict supervision it can be useful to put an armband around one ankle.

Dolphin (Reverse torpedo)

LOBSTER – STANDARD SCULL

The body is on the front, arms extended beyond the head. The head can be raised or with the face in the water. The wrists are hyper-extended, fingertips point upwards. Travel is feet first. In any scull where the arms are in advance of the head it is difficult to keep the feet up. In addition to using the back and tummy muscles it is not uncommon in the lobster to gently flutter kick.

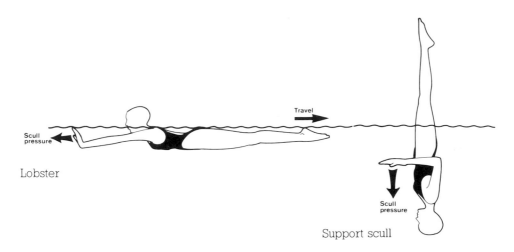

Lobster

Support scull

SUPPORT SCULL – FLAT SCULL

This is one of the most advanced sculls and takes a great deal of practice. The body is in the inverted-vertical position (see Chapter 4). An efficient scull will maintain height in the inverted position and will also help to raise the legs from the piked position (see Chapter 4) to the inverted vertical. The whole trunk should be firm with the head in line. The bottom should be firm too – it is common to say 'pinch pennies with your bottom'. The stability of the body can be aided considerably if the swimmer 'locks' the shoulder blades during the sculling. The elbows are tucked to the side of the body and bent to an angle of 90 degrees. The palms face the pool bottom. The flat sculling movement is used. The hands move away from the centre of the body and back. Pressure must be even and continuous. This scull can also be practised in the front-layout position, in which case the body will *travel*, feet first; and the tuck position (see Chapter 4).

PIKING SCULLS

Several sculls are used to enable the swimmer to achieve a pike position. Individuals must select the scull most suited to them. As the swimmer pikes, the feet and hips should remain at the water surface. The efficient piking scull enables the swimmer to travel along the surface to a 90-degree pike with the hips directly above the head.

It is important to appreciate that whichever scull is used for piking the swimmer must use the trunk to get a satisfactory 90 degree angle. As the swimmer sculls into the pike she must keep the trunk firm, bend at the hips and press the chest forwards, lock the shoulder blades and keep the head in line with the trunk. It is common for swimmers to tuck the head in during a pike and this causes the feet to sink; if the legs are then raised, as in a porpoise figure, the body will be piked if the legs are not lifted adequately, or arched if taken beyond the vertical.

Russian Scull

Starting in a front layout position, the arms are extended beyond the head, fingertips facing the pool bottom. The hands press back and up and somewhat outwards until they are just behind the shoulder line. The elbows are kept high, and the hands circle inwards like a small breaststroke arm pull until the little fingers almost touch and the palms face the bottom. The hands now scoop down and circle back towards the swimmer's face and the arms extend again. The scull is repeated until a 90-degree pike is achieved.

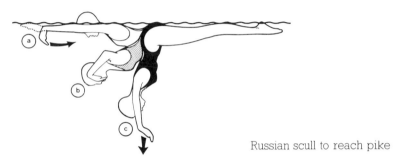

Russian scull to reach pike

Scooping

This is similar to a dog-paddle arm action in reverse. The arms push in an alternating manner up to the water surface and a pike is achieved.

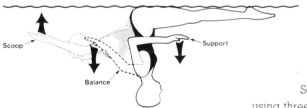

Scooping to pike,
using three different sculls

Reverse Scull

The arms are extended beyond the head and, as the hands reverse scull, the arms are pressed deeper into the water until a pike position is achieved.

Breaststroke Arm Action

Some swimmers use a small breaststroke-type arm action to cause the body to pike. It is similar to the first part of Russian scull, but does not have the scoop down and back towards the face as Russian scull does.

The 'Catch'

This movement is frequently used to get into a vertical position from a pike, eg, from a porpoise when the legs are along the surface and the head is inverted under the hips, which are at a 90-degree angle. To raise both legs to a vertical position above the head and out of the water requires a dynamic action. The arms are usually support sculling under the thighs and then they firmly press down and the swimmer lifts the legs into the vertical; the steadiness of the inverted position is controlled by quickly moving the hands outside the body and support sculling until everything is balanced again.

SCULLING PRACTICES

The following activities are suggestions for sculling practice. Pupils can learn the hand and arm techniques standing in shoulder-depth water before attempting to scull in the various body positions (see also Chapter 6). Some exercises require the execution of figures, such as tub and flamingo, and these are explained fully in Chapter 4. (TP=teaching points.)

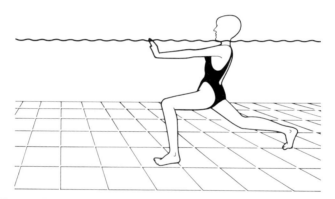

To practise the sculling action, stand in shoulder-depth water
and lean slightly backwards

1 On the back, standard scull. Travelling widthways across the pool.
TP The body is in an extended layout, the eyes looking up, arms by the sides with straight elbows.
2 On the back, standard scull. One knee bent.
TP Check that the bent leg thigh is vertical and the toe of the bent leg is on the inside of the horizontal leg. The horizontal leg stays at the surface.
3 On the back, standard scull. Alternate knee bends.
TP As for 2. Check control of knee bending and that the horizontal leg stays at the surface.
4 On the back, standard scull. Two legs bent, ie tub position.
TP Keep the head back and eyes up. The lower legs should be at the surface, thighs in a vertical line. Shorten the elbows during sculling.
5 On the back, standard scull. Single ballet leg position.

TP Body position as for 1. The horizontal leg stays at the surface while the other leg bends until the thigh is vertical and then extends the lower leg to vertical. Shorten the elbows and increase sculling speed.

6 On the back, standard scull into flamingo position.

TP As for 5, but the horizontal leg is placed knee to the chest with the foot of the lower leg at the water surface. The vertical leg meets the horizontal leg mid-calf.

7 On the back, standard scull. Double ballet-leg position.

TP As for 5, then slowly raise the second leg.

8 On the back, standard scull. Alternate leg raised 45 degrees.

TP Use tummy muscles during leg raising.

9 On the back reverse scull. Travelling widthways across the pool.

TP Body position as for 1.

10 On the front, reverse scull. Arms extended in advance of the head.

TP Hold the body firmly and keep the heels at the surface. Arms should be straight. Maintain continuity of sculling action.

11 On the back, flat scull. Toes 6in from wall.

TP Check that there is *no* travel. Maintain a firm even scull.

12 On the front, flat scull. Stationary canoe position. Nose 6in from wall.

TP Check that there is *no* travel. Maintain a firm even scull.

13 Canoe position (travelling), standard scull.

TP The body must be in a perfect line, and the elbows as straight as possible. Use an even and firm scull, and travel smoothly.

14 Canoe position (travelling), standard scull. One knee bent.

TP The heel of the horizontal leg should be at the surface. Keep the foot of the bent leg on the inside of the knee of the horizontal leg.

15 Canoe position (travelling), standard scull. One leg extended and vertically pointed downwards.

TP As for 14. Check that the vertical leg is straight and held firmly.

16 Torpedo scull, travelling feet first.

TP Keep the body extended. The arms are extended and narrow. The feet stay at the surface. Maintain smooth, even travel. The hands 'dust under the shelf'.

17 Dolphin scull (reverse torpedo).

TP Keep firm hands 'on the shelf'. Elbows are as straight as possible. Keep the feet up – if necessary, and under supervision, an armband around one ankle will help.

18 Dolphin scull (reverse torpedo). Towing a partner head first.

TP Partner to be towed in the tub position. The dolphin sculler places her feet around the waist of the tub partner.

19 Lobster scull, travelling feet first.

TP The arms are extended and fingertips raised. Travel smoothly, using a gentle kick if necessary.

20 Support scull, on the spot.

TP Hang from the poolside by the knees. Keep the back to the wall, head in line with the trunk. Elbows are held to the sides in a 90-degree bend, the palms of the hands face the pool bottom. Scull to centre body line and out so that lower arms touch the wall. Lock the shoulders as the arms press to the wall. Maintain an even scull inwards and outwards.

21 Support scull, face down. Travelling along the surface feet first.

TP Keep the face in the water, legs extended and heels at the surface. Elbows are to the sides in a 90-degree bend. Palms of hands face the direction opposite travel. Lock the shoulder blades on the outward and inward part of the scull. Maintain a smooth scull. Keep extended at the surface.

Sculling practice 20: support scull hanging from the poolside

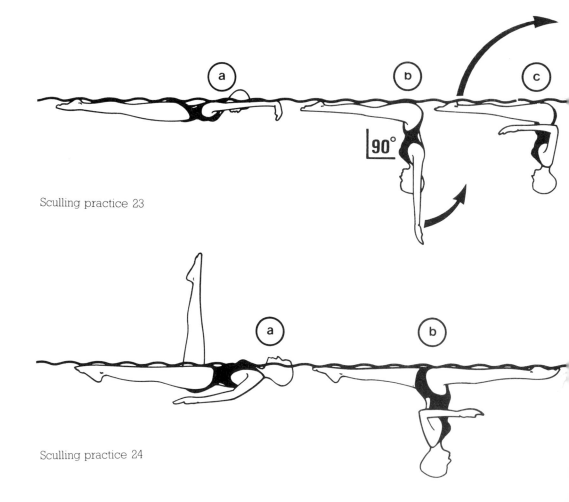

Sculling practice 23

Sculling practice 24

22 Support scull, submerging in vertical position. (Deep water required.)
TP The body must be vertical and firm, head in line with trunk. Keep the bottom firm. Sink just under water level. Elbows are bent and to the sides of the body in a 90-degree bend, palms face the water surface. Sculling action as for 20 and 21. If the scull is effective the body will submerge vertically.
23 Various body positions and sculling. Activities (a) to (e) can be repeated several times by tucking up and onto the front again after torpedo.
(a) reverse scull;
(b) use alternate scoops to get the body into a pike position;
(c) support scull in pike position;
(d) 'catch' and arch back with both legs arching over the water in a double walkover;
(e) torpedo scull.
24 Various body positions and sculling.
(a) single ballet leg, standard scull;
(b) back walkover, support scull;
(c) lobster scull;
(d) tuck up, flat scull and repeat from (a).

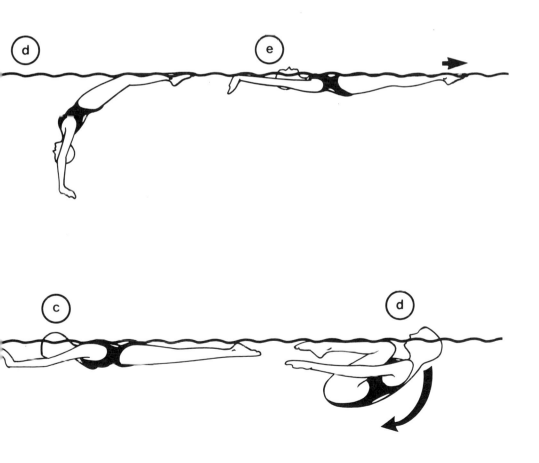

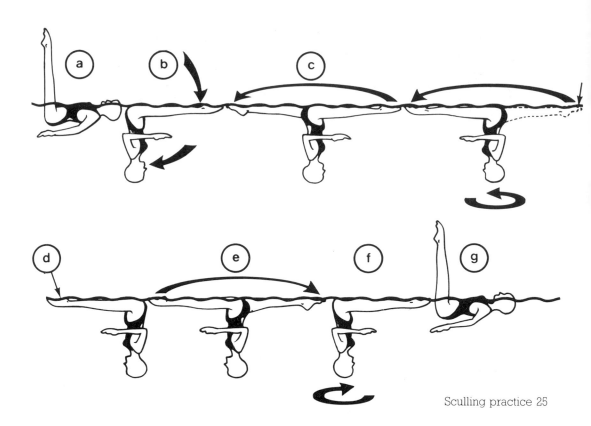

Sculling practice 25

25 Various body positions and sculling.
(a) double ballet leg, standard scull;
(b) rotate, scooping into support scull;
(c) support scull as one leg is swung sideways into the split position;
(d) bring the second leg round and use it to turn the trunk, support scull;
(e) swing the first leg sideways to where it originally started, support scull;
(f) swing the second leg to join the first leg and rotate trunk with second leg, support scull;
(g) use skipping action to rotate trunk to start position again. Go into standard scull and repeat from (a).

26 Standard, reverse and flat sculls to a drum beat. Work widthways across the pool, both individually and with partners.
Change from one scull to another on every heavy beat: eg 4 light beats, 1 heavy beat, change, etc. Synchronise with the beats and with partners.
27 Various sculls and changes of direction to music. Work widthways across the pool, both individually and with partners.
Change the direction of travel as dictated by the phrasing of the music: eg 8 beats, change, etc.

(*opposite*) Hand positions for standard scull (top), reverse scull (centre) and flat scull

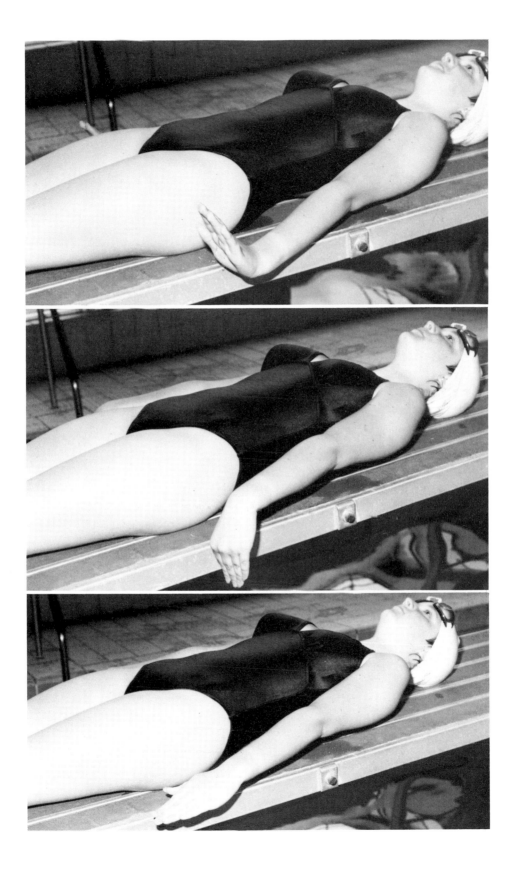

SCULLING SEQUENCES
Short Surface Sequence
This is a short and fairly simple surface routine for any number of swimmers swimming in ranks. Beats of the music are given (eg 1–8), and these should be counted to synchronise swimmers.

Music: 'La Vie En Rose' from a cassette called 'Melodies of the Centuries' by James Last, Polydor 315116.

1–8 (a) Flat scull on the spot.
1–8 (b) Standard scull.
1–8 (c) Reverse scull.
1–8 (d) Flat scull on the spot.
1–8 (e) Roll – canoe travel.
1–8 (f) On the spot canoe.
1–8 (g) Tuck – torpedo.
1–8 (h) 4 knee bends – standard scull.
1–8 (i) Flamingo.
1–8 (j) Tub, 4 quarter turns.
1–8 (k) Flat scull on the spot.
1–8 (l) 2 marlins.

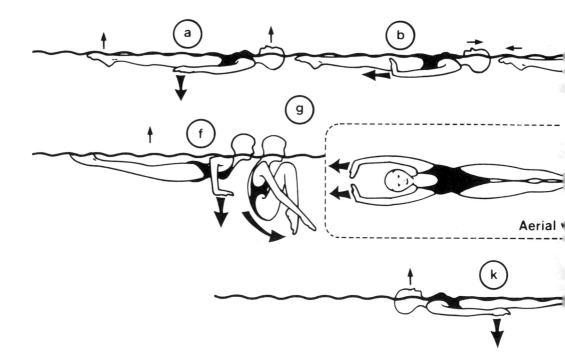

Sculling practice: short surface sequence

38

Flamingo position

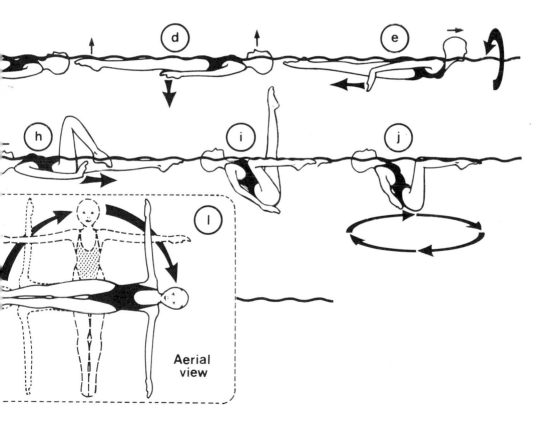

d

e

h

i

j

l

Aerial
view

Rank-formation Routine

This is a surface routine swum in ranks across the pool, for any number of swimmers. It is slightly more advanced. Beats of the music (eg 1–8) should be counted.

Music: 'Bone Shaker', played by Brendan Shine, from a cassette called 'My Old Country Home', Play LC1017.

      (a) Introduction on back.
1–8   (b) Standard scull.
1–8   (c) Reverse scull.
1–8   (d) Flat scull.
1–8   (e) Onto the front, canoe travel.
1–8   (f) Stationary canoe.

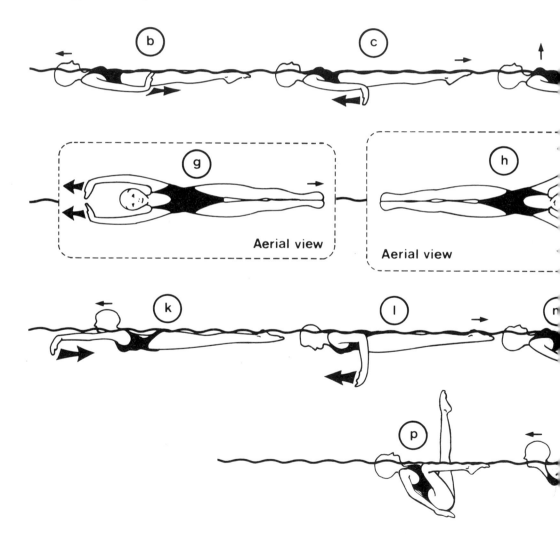

Sculling practice: rank-formation routine

1–8 (g) Turn onto the back, torpedo.
1–8 (h) Dolphin.
1–8 (i) Longitudinal roll onto front, lobster.
1–16 (j) Onto back and assume tub position.
1–8 (k) Move onto front (on the spot) then reverse scull.
1–8 (l) Support scull.
1–8 (m) Onto back, alternate knee bends.
1–8 (n) Ballet leg alternate.
1–8 (o) Alternate leg slightly raised.
1–8 (p) Flamingo.
1–8 (q) Onto front, canoe with one vertical leg.
1–4 (r) On back, flat scull.

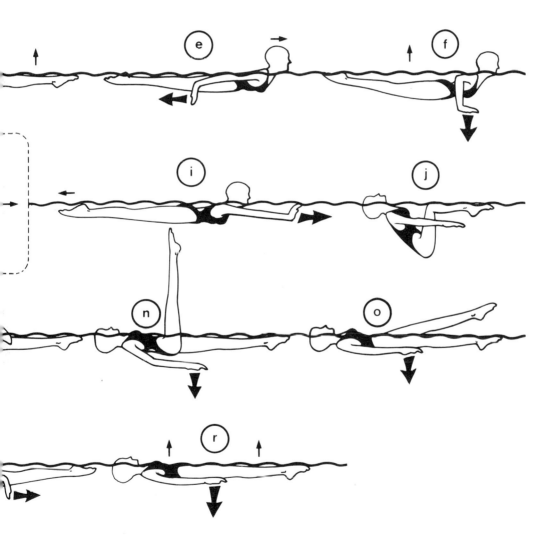

Double-circle Routine

This is a surface routine for twelve swimmers, using a double-circle formation. Beats of the music (eg 1–8) should be counted.

Music: 'Mary Rose' played by Elena Duran, from the cassette 'Viva Elena', RCAK 6030.

(a) Introduction. Back layout.

1–8 (b) Make 2 circles, feet pointing in, reverse scull.

1–8 (c) Get into tub position (1–2); 4 quarter turns, clockwise (3–6); straighten out (7–8).

1–8 (d) Standard scull out.

1–4 (e) Turn in straight position ready to travel head first round circle; travel clockwise.

5–8 (f) Into a flamingo position and execute 4 quarter turns.

1–8 (g) Tuck and face in, canoe position; canoe to centre of circle (1–4); tuck and rotate onto back (5–6); straighten (7); oyster (8).

1–2 (h) Surface, arms up (1); move arms to side, palms up (2).

1–8 (i) Swim breaststroke clockwise.

1–8 (j) Tuck legs through, then reverse scull anticlockwise; bend right knee (1–2), left knee (3–4) and repeat right (5–6), left (7–8).

1–2 (k) Turn feet in.

1–8 (l) Move in.

1–2 (m) Open legs (on surface).

3 (n) Close legs.

4 (o) Kick legs.

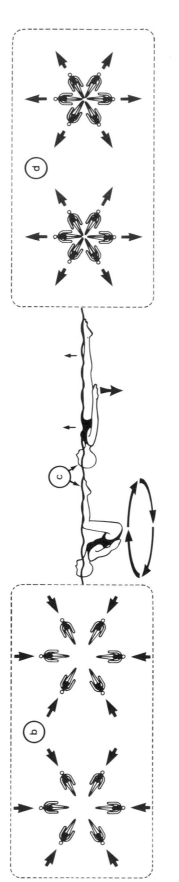

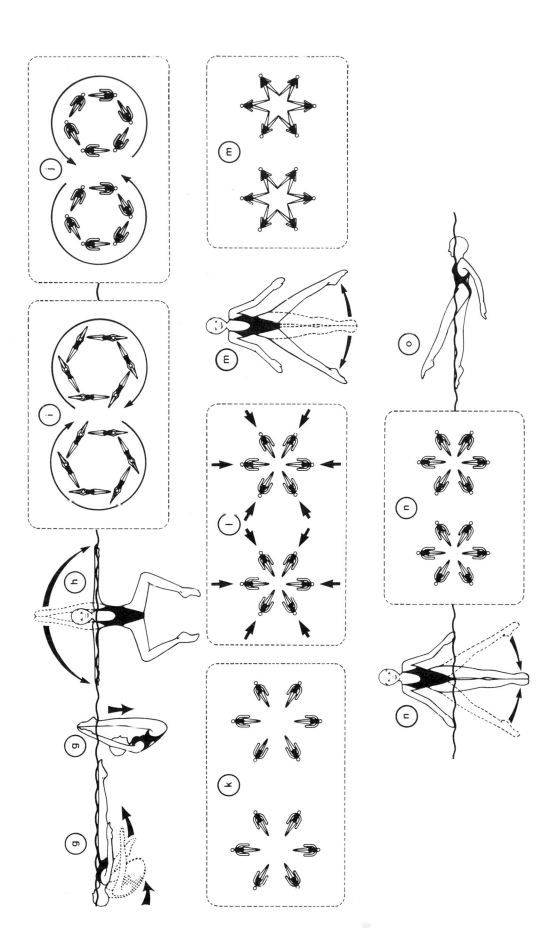

4 Figures and Positions

Figures are gymnastic movements in which the arms are used to propel, balance, turn, spin and control the body, while the legs and feet are usually used for 'effect' as the body is often upside down with only the legs showing above the water. Figures in synchronised swimming are listed into four categories:

Category I   Ballet-leg position figures.
Category II   Dolphin movement figures.
Category III   Somersaulting or piking movement figures.
Category IV   Any other figures not included in the above.

Every Olympic year FINA (Federation Internationale de Natation Amateur), the international body governing amateur swimming, chooses thirty-six figures from the four categories, placing them into six groups of six figures. In each group figures will be named from categories I to IV. Swimmers will know that for four years in competition these will be the figures they must perform.

Figures are tariffed according to their degree of difficulty, eg the relatively simple tub has a tariff of 1.1 and very difficult figures such as the castle are rated 2.3, but these do change, so tariffs are not given here. The simple figures are suitable for beginners but attaining proficiency in the high-tariffed figures takes years of training. When selecting the figures to suit the swimmers, the teacher must consider the ability and age of the pupils, and the water depth. Teachers and swimmers can experiment and invent their own figures which can evolve from tucks, pikes, straight positions, twisted positions, etc. A hybrid is a combination of several figures which results in an imaginative movement making sequence work more effective and creative.

Figures which are laid down by FINA should be performed slowly, with height and control. Each part of the figure must be 'clearly defined and in a uniform motion'. The leg and trunk movement must be exactly as set down by FINA though the arm action is optional. Sculling is an essential skill which enables the swimmer to perform figures more effectively.

LAYOUTS

Figures start in a layout position on the front, back or side. They finish in one of these three positions or upon submergence of the feet in an inverted-vertical position.

Back Layout

The swimmer lies extended horizontally on her back in the water. The toes, thighs, hips and face (eyes looking upwards) are near the water surface. The body should feel firm throughout and remain stationary.

The arm position is optional. In some figures the arms are held by the sides just under the hips and a firm flat scull is used. For dolphin figures the arms are usually extended beyond the head with a flat sculling movement and palms facing upwards just under the water surface.

Back layout (left), and front layout

Front Layout

The body is extended on the front with the heels, hips and head at the surface. The body must be firm and remain stationary, with the legs together and toes pointed. The face may be in the water or out. Arm position is optional. The arms can flat scull by the hip area or, if a swimmer is buoyant, are extended together beyond the head without sculling. A variation is the bent knee position which can be adopted for certain figures, eg the swordfish (see p62).

Side Layout

The body should initially be in the back layout with the arms extended, head squeezed between the arms, the legs stretched together and toes pointed, or the lower arm extended with the head resting on it and the upper arm placed close to the side, hand touching hip. The swimmer should practise stretching fully the side of the body she wishes to lie on. The body rotates to the fully stretched side. The body can be arched or extended, depending on the figure to be performed. The side layout is difficult to maintain and is usually required for shark figures.

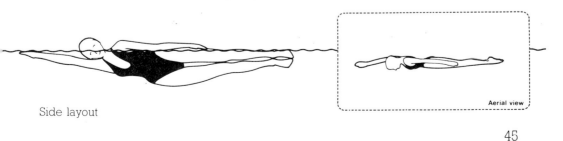

Aerial view

Side layout

BODY POSITIONS

The body positions which follow are essential during figure practice. The arm position is optional and will depend on the individual's buoyancy but should give maximum support.

Bent-knee Position

The body is in a back layout, front layout, or inverted-vertical position (see below). One foot is drawn alongside the opposite leg until the big toe of the bent leg is at or above the knee of the extended leg. In the back and front layouts the hips should be as near the water surface as possible. In the inverted-vertical position the knee is bent to the same line with the hip but the body can either be extended or arched.

As the leg bends, sculling speed increases. A flat (stationary) scull is used in the back and front layouts, and the support scull for the inverted-vertical position.

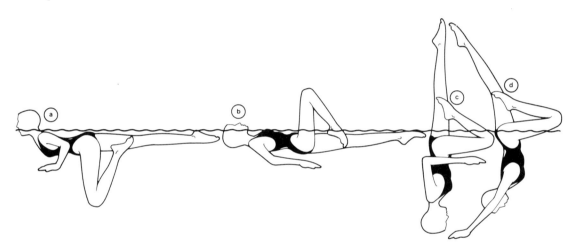

Bent-knee position in four variations: a) front layout, b) back layout, c) inverted-vertical position, d) arched inverted-vertical position

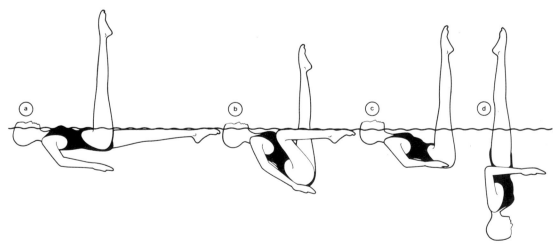

a) Single ballet-leg position, b) flamingo position, c) double ballet-leg position, d) inverted-vertical position

Single Ballet-leg Position
The swimmer is in a back layout. One leg assumes the bent knee position until thigh is vertical to trunk, and is then straightened until it is vertical. Toes, knee and thigh should be in a straight line. As the leg is returned to the bent-knee position the thigh must remain vertical. The big toe of the bent-knee leg draws a line along the horizontal leg as it is returned to the back layout.

Sculling speed increases during the bent-knee and extended-leg positions. The elbows are also slightly bent during this stage so that the support is higher up the body.

Flamingo Position
The single ballet-leg position is assumed. The horizontal leg is drawn along the surface and pressed to the chest. The bent leg should have mid-calf opposite the vertical leg. During the flamingo position the knee and foot of the bent leg should remain at the water surface. The head rests in the water, eyes up. A flat scull is used.

Double Ballet-leg Position
The flamingo position is assumed. The bent-knee leg assumes a vertical position alongside the other ballet leg. Both legs should be together, toes pointed and in line with the thighs. Speedier sculling is essential, with bent elbows. The face should be at the water surface.

Inverted-vertical Position
The body is extended with the head downwards and the trunk, hips and legs in a perfectly vertical line. This position can be reached from a pike position, as in the Porpoise figure (p62). Height is desirable and the water line should in any case be between hips and ankle. A support scull is used to the side of the body, see Chapter 3.

Tub Position
From the back layout the knees, lower legs and feet are drawn along the water surface until the thighs are vertical and above the hips, which lower into the water as the knees bend.

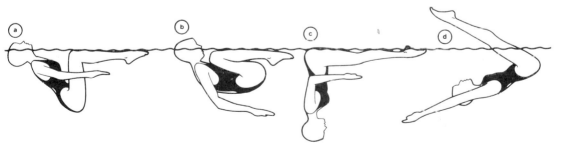

a) Tub position, b) tuck position, c) and d) front and back pike positions

Compact-tuck Position (see p47)

The compact tuck is used during back and forward rotation. From a back layout, the knees are tucked to the chest, legs together and feet wrapped around the bottom. The head is tucked in and the back rounded. The inverted compact-tuck is the same shape but with the head underwater; it can be reached from the front or back layout and uses the support scull to keep stationary (see somersault front tuck, and kip).

Inverted compact-tuck position, showing the support scull

Front-pike Position (see p47)

From the front layout, the body is bent at the hips to form a 90-degree angle. The legs are straight and together, toes are pointed. The head is in line with the trunk and the back straight.

Back-pike Position (see p47)

This is a closed-pike position. The body is bent sharply at the hips and the trunk is straight. The legs are straight together and close to the chest, keeping the position as compact as possible. The toes are pointed.

Crane Position

From a front-pike position one leg is raised vertically. There should be a 90-degree angle between the horizontal leg which is parallel to the water surface and the trunk. The head, hips and vertical leg should be in a straight line. Height is desirable. A support scull is used under the horizontal leg.

Fishtail Position

The body position is the same as for the crane. The foot of the horizontal extended leg is at the water surface even if the hips are not.

48

Split Position

The trunk is in the inverted position and as straight as possible. A support scull is used. Shoulders are under the hips and the head is in line with the trunk. The legs are split forwards and backwards with the hips as near the water surface as possible. The feet and legs should be extended horizontally along the surface.

Knight Position (Castle)

The trunk is inverted and arched. The head and shoulders should be under the hips with the head vertical. One leg is vertical and the other leg extended backwards with the foot at the surface as close to the horizontal position as possible.

a) Crane position, b) fishtail position, c) split position, d) knight position

BASIC MOVEMENTS

Twists (see p50)

A twist is a rotation with the body held in the inverted-vertical position, and maintaining equal height throughout the movement. The water level is between the ankles and hips, and the head must be in line with the trunk. It is possible to perform:

A half twist of 180 degrees.
A full twist of 360 degrees.
A twirl – this is a rapid rotation of 180 degrees at the height of the vertical.

The arm position is optional. One arm needs to maintain height and stability and the other to aid the rotation. The swimmer usually sculls with the arms above the head or in the support scull near the waist/hip line. Sculling must be smooth and even to ensure a stable twist.

Spins (see p50)

A spin is a *descending rotation* executed in one uniform motion. The body is in the inverted-vertical position. It must be absolutely straight and firm with the head in line with the trunk.

All spins should start at the full height of the vertical. In both 180-degree and 360-degree spins the movement must be completed by the time the heels reach the surface of the water. In the *continuous spin* the movement continues until the heels drop below the surface of the water, after completing a rotation of at least 360 degrees.

a) Twist, b) spin

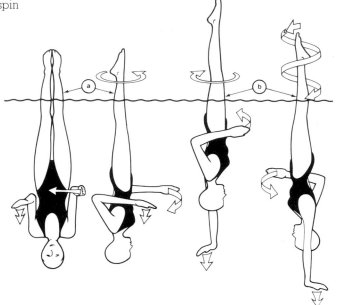

Twist Spin
In this movement a twist of 180 degrees is completed at the height of the vertical followed by a descending spin of at least 180 degrees. The spin continues until the heels drop below the surface of the water.

The arm position during spins is optional. One arm maintains stability and height and the other initiates the spin. The arms are either beyond the head or at the mid-trunk area.

Very buoyant swimmers often find it difficult to descend. It helps to exhale slightly. The buoyant swimmer also surfaces rapidly after a figure and, to slow the process, exhalation again steadies the movement.

FIGURE PRACTICE
The following figures are suggested as a starting point for the teacher. They all require a great deal of practice in order to be performed correctly. Most require deeper water and the teacher should be very careful to ensure that the depth is adequate for the activity. Once mastered, these figures have an infinitely variable number of applications. (TP=teaching points.)

Tub

1 Back layout at the water surface.

TP Body extended, eyes up, hips and feet up. Use firm flat scull.

2 Tub position, rotate 360 degrees.

TP Keep eyes up. Draw knees and feet along water surface until the thighs are vertical. Speed up flat scull. To initiate rotation: flat scull with the hand on the side opposite the direction of rotation. Place other hand in standard-scull position, pushing in the opposite direction.

3 Extend into back layout.

TP Take knees and feet *along* the water surface to find back layout.

Tub

Oyster

1 Back layout at the water surface.

TP Body extended, eyes up, hips and feet up. Use firm flat scull.

2 Transfer the arms to a position in advance of the head.

TP Maintain firm flat-scull rhythm. Turn hands firmly, palms up. Keep body stationary.

3 Sharp compact pike.

TP Scoop arms up and forwards. Keep the head in line with the arms. Pike at hips. The hands touch the top of the ankles or the toes. Point toes.

4 Submerge in closed pike.

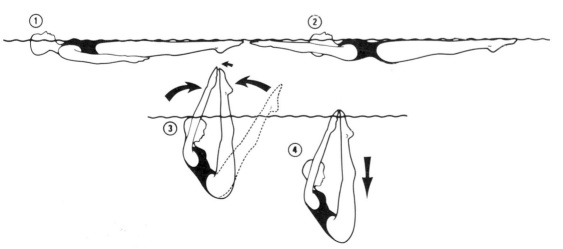

Oyster

Shark

1 Hold side or rail of pool, with body in side layout. Push off and extend the upper arm like a shark's fin.

TP Keep head back, hips forward, legs together and feet stretched. Scull with under arm by hip, or scoop.

2 Side layout in shallow end, back arched.

3 Work with a partner from opposite sides of the pool. Push off, scull in shark position, passing partner at pool centre.

Somersault Back Tuck

1 Back layout.

TP Keep eyes up, hips and feet up, arms by *side* and body extended. Use firm flat scull.

2 Compact tuck.

TP Knees and feet start along surface. Knees bend to chest and then to nose. Wrap feet round the seat. Use firm flat scull.

3 Rotate back.

TP Keep head tucked in, body compact and back rounded. Use flat scull and/or gentle small forward scoops with arms as the body rotates back. Feet just break the water surface during rotation.

4 Nearing end of rotation.

TP Keep body compact.

5 Final stage of compact tuck.

TP Keep body compact. Maintain flat scull.

6 Final back layout.

TP Extend body slowly from compact shape. Knees and feet travel to extended position along surface. Flat scull.

Somersault Front Tuck

Before commencing this figure, practise the mushroom float: take deep breath and move slowly into the inverted compact-tuck position, round back and keep head tucked in. Use support scull.

1 Front layout.

TP Keep body and head steady, with hips raised and feet at surface. Flat scull, remaining on the spot.

2 Get into inverted compact tuck at the surface.

TP Maintaining scull, draw feet slowly along the surface. As knees move close to chest, tuck head in.

3 Rotate forwards in compact shape.

TP Arms skip *back* to initiate forward rotation. Maintain tuck shape. Wrap feet round the seat.

4 Complete rotation and extend to front layout.

TP Flat scull as tuck is nearing completion. Keep feet at the surface and proceed slowly.

5 Finish in front layout.

Shark

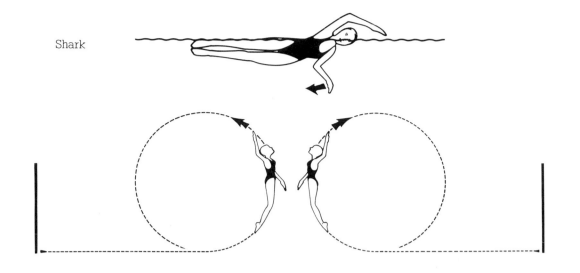

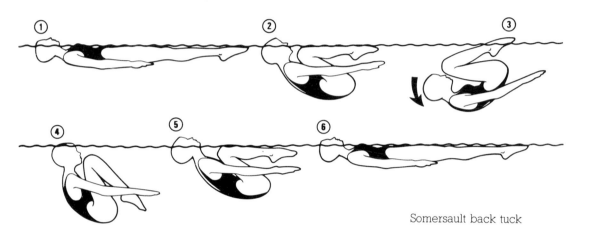

Somersault back tuck

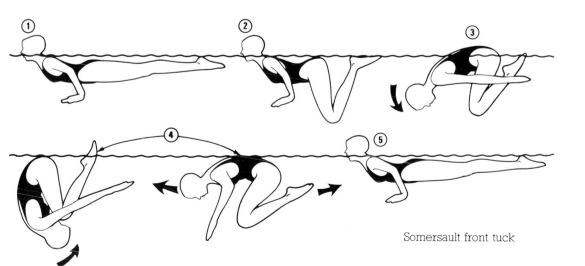

Somersault front tuck

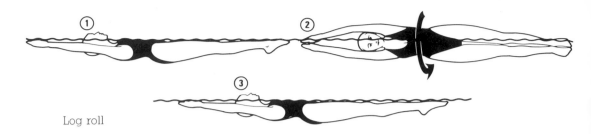

Log roll

Log Roll
Practise initiating body roll before attempting the figure.
1 Back layout.
TP Fully extend body and keep head in line. Face, feet and thighs should be at the water surface. Extend arms in advance of the head, with hands held palms up and thumbs side by side.
2 Extended body roll at the surface (one revolution).
TP Keep *one* side of the body extended and feet at the surface. No kicking is allowed. Glue ear to the extended arm. (NB: If the extension of one side of the body doesn't initiate a roll, pike down slightly at the hips and push the hips sideways opposite the direction of the roll. Glue ear to the extended arm on the side you wish to roll to. Keep the legs and arms near the surface throughout, and after pike and sideways push keep the hips near the surface.)
3 Finish in back layout.

Marlin
Imagine a large circle at the water surface, divided into four quarters.
1 Back layout with arms in a T position.
TP Keep the eyes up, hips and feet up and the palms of the hands down.
2 Quarter turn round circle with full twist of the body.
TP Lie with the head glued to the centre of the circle. Arms are held spread and straight near the surface (no sculling is allowed) and must remain equidistant throughout. Reach across the body with one arm to initiate rotation of the trunk. The other arm moves to balance it. The trunk rotates at the surface for *one whole rotation*. The arms, looking like aeroplane wings, finish on the surface still in a T position. At the end of the movement, one quarter of the imaginary circle is completed.
3 Finish in back layout with arms in a T position.

Somersault Front Pike
1 Starting in front layout, scull forwards 18in along the surface, and extend arms forward.
TP As for somersault front tuck, keep body extended and feet at the surface. *Gently* take arms forwards and use flat scull during transfer.
2 Reverse scull travelling forward 18in along water surface.
TP Continue arm/hand movement.

Marlin

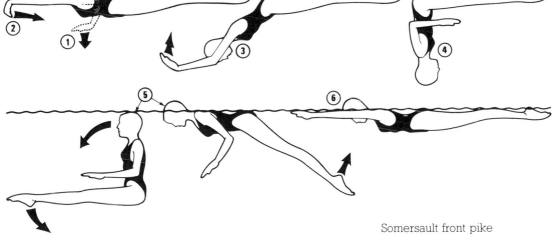

Somersault front pike

3 Scoop arms slightly up to initiate pike position.

TP Keep feet at the surface and head steady.

4 Get into 90-degree pike position.

TP Support scull to maintain pike.

5 Rotate forwards in open-pike position.

TP Keep head in line with trunk. As body moves forwards, arms skip back. Legs are extended with feet and knees together. The feet just break the water surface during the rotation. Keep the movement smooth and slow.

6 Finish in front layout.

TP Use flat scull as extended lower legs are raised to the surface. Head and trunk should finish in line with the water surface. Keep the body steady.

Somersault Back Pike

1 Back layout at water surface.

TP Keep body extended, eyes up, hips and feet up. Use firm flat scull.

2 Arms flat scull to sides of shoulders.

TP Maintain firm scull rhythm. Keep the body stationary during the transfer of the arms. Turn the hands firmly, palms up.

3 Initiate compact-pike position.

TP Scoop arms up and flat scull firmly to a position in advance of the head. Work on achieving a sharp bend at the hips, getting the pike as compact as possible.

4 Rotate in pike, near water surface.

TP Keep position compact. Flat scull arms to a support position by the hips in order to control continued pike rotation. Work on smooth transfer of hands.

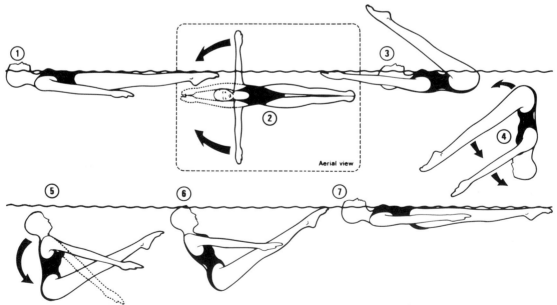

Somersault back pike

5 Conclude pike.

TP Keep position compact. Flat scull arms into extended position. The head and feet should break the surface together. Move slowly into the final layout.

6 Final back layout (count 6).

TP Keep eyes up, hips and feet up, legs extended and body stationary.

Dolphin (see p58)

First, practise travelling along the water surface using the dolphin scull and keeping a flat, streamlined body position.

1 Starting in back layout, travel 18in at the surface.

TP Keep body extended, eyes up, hips and feet up. Arms should be extended in advance of the head. Raise the wrists, keep hands firm with palms up and fingers together. Use firm dolphin scull to travel.

2 Arch, head first, and begin to submerge, following the shape of a 9ft circle.

TP Keep the dolphin scull going. Arch the back and lock shoulder blades. Hips are raised, legs and feet together. Keep the feet in the water.

3 Travel down, arch at the second corner and travel across the base of the circle.

TP As the body reaches the second corner the arms transfer to a position by the hips and the hands now use a standard scull. The body is held slightly arched to move along the base of the circle in a travelling canoe position.

4 Arch at the third corner and travel towards the surface.

TP Arms are still by the hips using the standard scull.

5 Round over the fourth corner and surface.

TP Appear quietly at the surface. Control breathing.

6 Travel along the surface until the feet reach the point where the head submerged at the beginning of the dolphin circle, finishing in a steady final back layout.

TP Use steady, smooth standard scull to travel until final position is reached. Then hold back layout extended and stationary, using firm flat scull.

Dolphin Foot First (see p58)

1 Starting in back layout, travel along surface feet first (1ft to 18in).

TP Keep body extended, eyes up, hips and feet up. With hands just under hips, use firm reverse scull to travel.

2 Arch, feet first, and begin to submerge, following the shape of a 9ft circle.

TP Keep the reverse scull going, hands behind hips. Keep hips up and head back. Lock the shoulders and small of the back.

3 Travel down 8 to 9ft and arch at second corner, continuing 3 to 4ft along the bottom of the circle.

TP Use a support scull or alternate scoops up towards the water surface. Continuity of rhythm is vital.

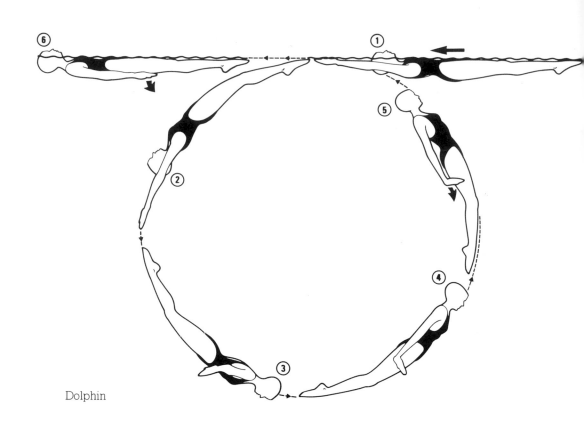

Dolphin

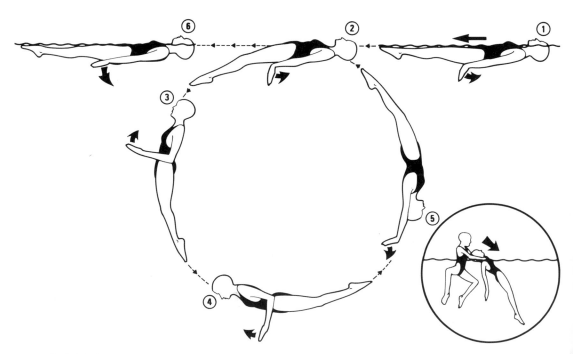

Dolphin foot first

4 Arch round third corner and straighten slightly to travel to surface.

TP Continue to use support scull or alternate scoop. (If travel towards the surface is too rapid, blow *out* slightly.)

5 Circle over fourth corner and travel along surface in torpedo scull until the head reaches the point where the feet submerged into the first corner.

TP Gently transfer arms beyond the head to torpedo scull. To stop, place the hands in the dolphin-scull position and then use a firm flat scull to maintain back layout.

6 Final back layout.

TP Use firm flat scull with the arms extended beyond the head.

(NB: Any swimmer finding the submerging difficult can be aided by a partner. The partner places both arms on the swimmer's shoulders and pushes her hard downwards into the foot-first submerging phase.)

Single Ballet Leg

1 Back layout.

TP The head rests in the water, eyes up. Keep the legs extended and the hips and feet up. Use a firm flat scull with the arms by the sides.

2 Bend one leg slowly until the thigh is vertical.

TP The elbows bend as the lever is shortened during a speeded-up flat scull. Work the tummy muscles hard to keep the horizontal (non-ballet) leg at the surface. (If the horizontal leg sinks put an arm-band around the ankle.) The foot of the ballet leg draws a line along the horizontal leg as the bend is executed.

3 Extend ballet leg to vertical.

TP Check that the thigh remains vertical during movement. Lock the knee and point the toes.

4 Return the ballet leg to a bent-knee position.

TP Keep the thigh vertical during the movement and return the leg slowly, tightening the tummy muscles to cope.

5 Finish in back layout.

TP Extend the bent leg slowly along the horizontal leg. Use a firm flat scull.

Single ballet leg

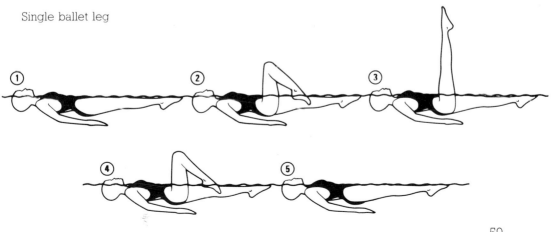

Kip

Before trying this figure, practise the tuck and extending the legs while holding onto the trough or rail (see photographs).

1 Back layout.

TP The head rests in the water, eyes up. Keep the legs extended and the hips and feet up. Use a firm flat scull.

2 Tuck up into a compact shape.

TP Speed up the flat scull. Hands stay by the hips. Wrap feet around the seat.

3 In the compact tuck, rotate back and upside down.

TP When the *lower* legs point directly up, the hands, which have been flat sculling by the hips, move to support scull under the knees.

4 Extend the legs to vertical.

TP Use a support scull as the legs extend. (As the legs arrive at the vertical position the scull moves wider to the side of the trunk.) Lower legs should remain vertical during extension and the inverted vertical.

5 Descend *slowly* in the inverted-vertical position.

TP Keep the body extended with the head in line. Keep the legs together and stretch the toes. Use a support scull.

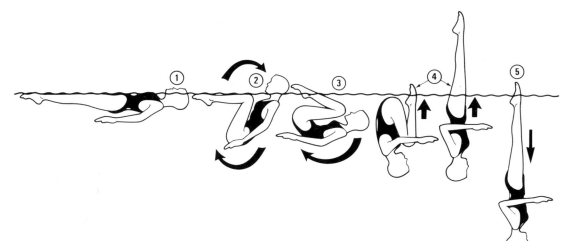

Kip

Practice for kip: compact tuck while holding trough/rail

Practice for kip: from tuck, extend legs horizontally

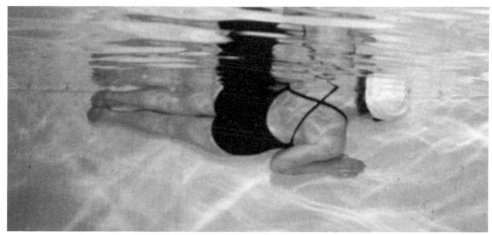

Practice for kip: compact-tuck position, upside down, holding trough/rail

Swordfish

1 Front layout.

TP Keep the body extended and the legs stretched, with the heels at the surface. The face may be in or the chin on the surface of the water. Use a firm flat scull.

2 Bend one leg until the foot reaches the knee of the horizontal leg.

TP Keep the straight leg stretched and at the water surface. Draw a line along the straight leg with the big toe of the bending leg. Use a flat scull.

3 Arch the back and lift the legs over the water surface, drawing an arc with the foot of the extended leg.

TP Keep the head back, shoulders locked and hips forward. The hands scoop down and forwards from the hips and stop level with the shoulders, then flat scull back to the hips and repeat. OR: use alternate scoops similar to a reverse dog paddle. (NB: As the extended leg reaches the vertical in its route over the surface, support scull hard directly by the side of the body.)

4 As extended leg arrives at the surface, return bent leg to horizontal.

TP Keep the back arched and the extended leg horizontal at the surface. Straighten the bent leg, drawing the big toe carefully along the extended leg. Use a support scull.

5 With both legs together, arch body up and travel along the surface to the final back layout.

TP Keep both feet at the water surface. Torpedo scull out along surface. Bring head in line with the trunk. Stop travel by reverse scull hand position into firm flat scull to keep body stationary.

6 Finish in back layout.

Porpoise

1 From a stationary front layout, extend the arms forwards and travel along the surface for 1ft to 18in.

TP Keep the body extended and hips and heels at the surface. The head may be raised or the face kept in the water. Commence with a flat scull to keep the body stationary, then scull arms firmly to a position in advance of the body. Reverse scull to travel along the surface.

2 Bend body into a 90-degree pike.

TP Take the arms a few inches under the water and either use scooping scull up OR reverse scull OR Russian scull. The hips and legs stay at the surface. Use a firm trunk press into the pike. Keep the head in line with the trunk. Lock the shoulders and press the small of the back forwards.

3 Raise both legs to the inverted-vertical position.

TP Support scull with hands under the thighs. Press down hard to lift both legs to the vertical. 'Pinch pennies' with the bottom. Keep the head in line with the trunk and the body extended.

4 Descend in the inverted-vertical position.

TP After pressing down to lift the legs, control the lift by a support scull to the side of the body and descend *slowly*.

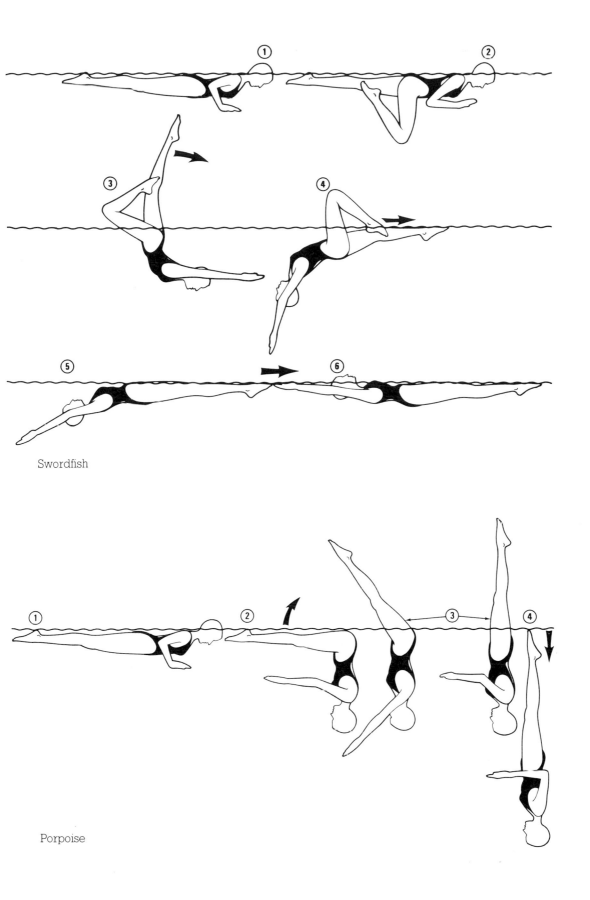

Swordfish

Porpoise

Walkover Back

1 Back layout.

TP Keep eyes, hips and feet up. Hands flat scull firmly, moving to a position in advance of the head.

2 Travel along the surface and arch body slightly, submerging until the head is under the hips.

TP Use dolphin scull.

3a Lift one leg in extended position.

3b Draw an arc over the water to reach the split position.

TP Use a support scull as the leg lifts. Keep the head back.

4 Lift the second leg over the water. The body is now in a pike.

TP Use a support scull. The head should now be in line with the trunk.

5 From the pike position, bring the trunk into line with the legs, travel out feet first along the surface and finish in a stationary front layout. To travel, use the lobster scull, keeping the face in the water.

TP Use a support scull to raise trunk. To finish, raise the head and use a flat scull to keep the body stationary. The feet should be at the surface.

Somersub

1 Front layout.

TP Keep the head steady and the hips and feet up. Use a flat scull to maintain a stationary position.

2 Travel into a 90-degree pike position.

TP As for porpoise (see p62).

3 Rotate the body in the 90-degree pike position.

TP The legs should end up in a vertical position where the hips were at the water surface, with the water level between the knees and ankles. The arms use a firm scull to control the rotation. To hold the vertical position and prevent the body sinking, the hands flat scull *under* the hips. Keep the trunk straight, with the head in line and the shoulders locked.

4 Lower one leg in the extended position until it is in line with the horizontal trunk.

TP The lowered leg and the trunk must be parallel to the water surface. The other leg remains in a ballet-leg position. Use a combination of firm upward scoops and a flat scull to keep the body submerged and steady.

5 Rise to surface.

TP Keep head, trunk and horizontal leg in line as they travel to the surface. The vertical leg maintains the ballet-leg position. Use a flat scull.

6 Return ballet leg to horizontal, via bent-knee position.

TP Use the tummy muscles to control lowering of the leg. The toe of the ballet leg draws a line along the horizontal leg as it returns to the back layout. Use a firm flat scull.

7 Finish in a stationary back layout.

TP Keep the eyes, hips and feet up. Flat scull by the hips.

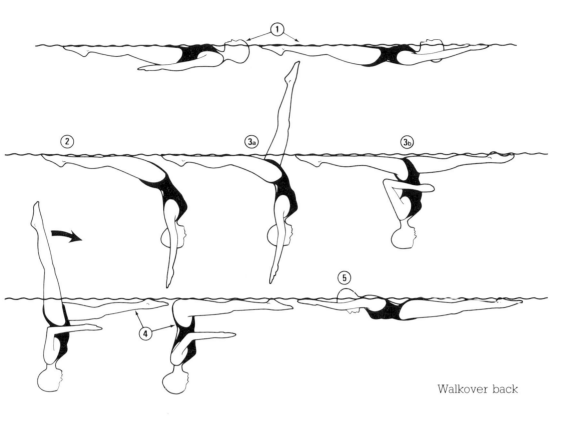

Walkover back

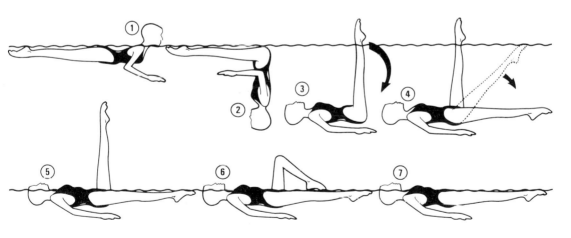

Somersub

Eiffel Tower

1 Back layout.

TP Keep the body extended and the hips and eyes up. Use a flat scull.

2 Raise one leg to the single ballet-leg position.

TP As for single ballet leg (see p59).

3 Take the ballet leg across the horizontal leg to the surface.

TP Use a flat scull. Keep the eyes up. Maintain a 90-degree angle between the horizontal leg and the ballet leg. Keep the horizontal leg at the surface by pushing it up against the ballet leg; the ballet leg pushes *down*, so the action is similar to that of a pair of scissors. The horizontal leg must be in line with the trunk.

4 Move the trunk downwards to a front-pike position and at the same time move the ballet leg across the water surface to meet the non-ballet leg which must remain stationary.

TP The trunk should be firm with the head in line. Scoop scull to get into pike. The arms steady the pike position by momentarily sculling behind the back.

5 Raise the non-ballet leg to the vertical.

TP Use a support scull.

6 Raise the ballet leg to the vertical.

TP Use support scull.

7 Descend in the inverted-vertical position.

TP Keep the body firm and the head in line. Use a support scull as the body descends.

Eiffel tower, showing 90-degree angle between legs in stage 3

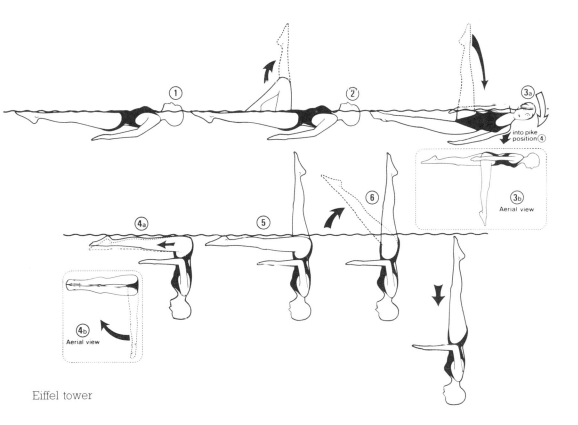

Eiffel tower

Catalina Reverse

1 Front layout.

TP Keep the head steady and hips and feet up. Use a flat scull.

2 Travel into a 90-degree pike position, as for porpoise (see p62).

TP The bottom, legs and feet travel along the surface. For travel, use a reverse scull. To pike, use a scoop scull.

3 Raise one leg to assume a crane position.

TP Use a support scull.

4 Execute a reverse catalina rotation to a ballet-leg position (see diagram).

TP The water level must remain constant on the vertical leg during the rotation. (NB: It often helps if the teacher holds the vertical leg and rotates it. This gives the pupil the idea of holding the vertical leg in position during the rotation.) Hands are near hips to support and flat scull. Trunk rises to surface.

5 As body reaches surface, hold the single ballet-leg position.

TP The horizontal leg should be extended and pressed down. The trunk pushes down. Lock the shoulder blades and keep the head and trunk in line with the horizontal leg. Use a firm flat scull.

6 Lower the ballet leg.

TP Use a firm flat scull.

7 Finish in back layout.

TP Use a firm flat scull.

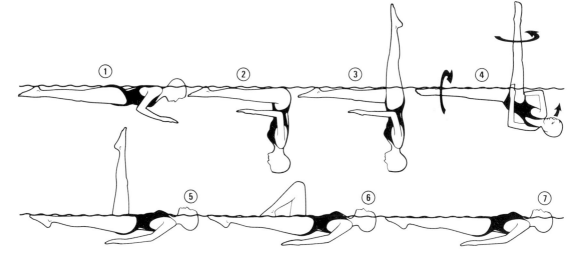

Catalina reverse

5 Routines, Choreography and Competitions

SEQUENCE WORK AND CHOREOGRAPHY

The sequence or routine comprises figures and variations, linked by strokes and sculling and performed to a musical accompaniment. When choreographing a sequence there are certain factors to be considered: the figures chosen and the ability of the swimmers to perform them; the pool pattern; music and its interpretation; timing; formations; presentation and costume.

Figures and Strokes

Swimmers should use a wide range of figures with varying degrees of difficulty eg ballet leg, dolphin figures, perhaps twists and spins. Some swimmers use just one type of figure, eg those incorporating splits, but this can make a sequence fairly repetitive and boring. Each figure or part of a figure should be well executed with much attention paid to technical detail. The strokes and other linking movements should be well performed and make effective transitions. The swimmer can use front crawl, back crawl and breaststroke, and there are infinite variations of these.

Whatever the content of the sequence, it must be applicable to the age and ability of the swimmers. A simple sequence, especially for young swimmers, can be very effective and is better than a vastly complicated, poorly executed one. In duets and teams it is essential to use movements that can be well performed by *all* swimmers. It is pointless choosing movements that are beyond the capabilities of one or two swimmers because the overall effect of the routine will be spoilt. The team routines given later in this chapter are fairly basic, aimed at a cross-section of abilities. The duet given was choreographed for two girls of grade 2 ability.

Pool Pattern

It is important for a swimmer to move around the pool as much as possible. A routine becomes very static and boring if the performer stays rooted to the spot. Changes of direction create interest and variety and they can be made within a figure or during an underwater phase. The whole pool should be used and the swimmer should avoid following the same route twice. Obviously the size of the pool and the depth of the water will influence the choreography.

(*top*) Chain dolphin; (*above*) Matching shapes in a duet

Music and its Interpretation

The music chosen must be appropriate to the mood of the sequence and the age, ability and personality of the swimmer. The soloist has the greatest freedom of choice, because she doesn't have to consider other swimmers. A very young soloist will not look right using music which is sombre and dull. Something bright and cheerful would be better, ie polkas, waltzes, light orchestral. The more advanced soloist can choose a more difficult accompaniment. Duets and teams should choose music that suits both or all swimmers and is relatively easy to count to so that all can keep in time; marches are ideal. In all sequences contrasting rhythms, some fast and some slow, not only add interest from an audience point of view, but also give the swimmers a bit of a breather and a change of pace.

The music should have an exciting beginning to capture the attention of the audience and also build up to a grand finale and climactic end. It is very frustrating if a routine just fades out because audience and judges do not know whether it has actually finished or not!

Effective interpretation of the music is the essence of a good routine. Sequences should be swum with feeling and reflect the mood that is portrayed in the music. A joyous and lively tune should inspire correspondingly energetic movements in the water. Similarly, slow and sad passages should be interpreted by gentle movements, and certain pieces might suggest twists or spins.

Synchronisation with music is interesting. The swimmers must start and end with the accompaniment. In some sequences the music seems merely to provide background noise and is not 'used' by the swimmers. In a good sequence every beat is accounted for and every swimmer knows what is happening with every beat. In duets and teams, the swimmers should be so sure of what they are doing that they could swim with their eyes closed and still be in time with their partners and the music. It takes only one swimmer to be slightly out of synchronisation for the whole routine to be ruined.

Timing

The timing for each routine is vital. In competitive synchro the solo routine has a time allowance of 3 minutes and 30 seconds, plus or minus 15 seconds; a duet has a timing of 4 minutes, plus or minus 15 seconds; and a team routine has a timing of 5 minutes, plus or minus 15 seconds. Within these times, 20 seconds are allowed for deckwork. Obviously, if creating sequences for displays or simply for enjoyment there is no limit on time.

Group formation

Formations

Formations are limited in duet routines but the swimmers can work side by side, one in front of the other, one diagonally in front of the other, facing each other or facing away. In duets, assisted lifts, where one partner lifts the other, can be dramatic. Partners can also support each other, and make interesting, complementary shapes. In team routines, many different formations and formation changes can be used to great effect (see p25). If required, there are many ways in which the swimmers can link themselves together in formation, eg toes or shoulders, clasping hands – depending on the demands of the routine.

Presentation and Costume

This really is the icing on the cake but both the manner and appearance of the swimmers are important. Swimmers should show 'presence' on the poolside even before entering the water. They should be confident and composed and take pride in their performances. There is nothing worse than swimmers who slouch onto the poolside, fiddle with costumes and noseclips and then give a very introverted performance. Personalities need to be stamped onto routines and the extrovert has a great advantage. Neglect of these fine details will spoil the overall effect of a routine.

Costumes can do much to enhance a sequence. Colour is vitally important. If a routine is lively and gay then red, bright pink, or electric blue may match the mood. If the routine is slower and sad, more subtle colours may be a wiser choice, ie pale blue or green. Certain colours look good in

Legs linked for a duet movement

water and others look very dull. Many swimmers choose a plain costume and then decorate it themselves to suit the routine that they are performing. This is fine and we see some highly original ideas. Too much decoration, however, can look messy and can detract from a sequence. The costume should be a one-piece and should be devoid of openwork. It should be tested in the water before its debut to ensure that it is not transparent when wet! It is very embarrassing to discover that problem when performing in front of an audience.

Any headgear that is worn should match the swimmer's costume and must be waterproof. It should not restrict movement in any way. Some head-dresses, if they are too heavy or bulky, can throw the swimmer off balance, particularly when she is upside-down in the water. Headgear must be securely fixed so that it cannot slip or be dislodged during a routine; nothing looks worse than a swimmer who surfaces with everything awry!

Make-up must be waterproof and should not be overdone. A little cheek colour, along with a touch of eye-shadow and lipstick, is all that is needed. The 'painted-doll' effect is not pleasing and is unnecessary. Make-up is used simply to enhance natural features and to ensure that the swimmer doesn't look pale to an audience who may be situated some distance away.

Hair must be off the face, preferably in a bun of some sort to keep it neat and tidy. Most swimmers these days use gelatine to control their hair and this should be applied at least one hour before a performance to ensure that it has time to set. The gelatine 'melts' out of the hair fairly easily in a hot shower afterwards.

Partner support using complementary shapes

FLOATING FORMATIONS

These are very effective and rely totally on sculling and changes of formation. There are many patterns that can be created in this way. Below, I have illustrated a few in a floating formation routine for eight swimmers to a piece of music called 'Canale Grande' by Rondo Veneziano. Beats of the music (eg 1–8) should be counted.

Beats of music	Action	Pool Pattern
1–3 Intro-duction	Scull on the spot, making a circle with feet to the centre.	
1–4	Alternate swimmers standard scull one body length.	
5–8	The other four swimmers scull and travel clockwise until their heads meet the feet of the first four.	
1–8	Whole circle maintains position and rotates 180 degrees anti-clockwise.	
1–4	Reverse scull into a line, alternating heads and feet.	

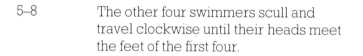

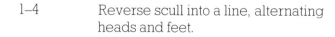

74

5–8	Scull, opening legs to create a wide trellis effect.	
1–4	Scull, closing together again.	
Trill passage in music	Standard scull (quickly) and move feet to feet with a partner.	
1–8	Scull and move into a double diamond formation.	
1–4	Move into a rectangular shape.	
5–8	Everyone reverse scull and submerge 'over a barrel'.	
1–8	Surface head first and feet first alternately and standard and reverse scull into a large open circle.	

ENTRIES

A synchronised swimming routine may start on land or in the water. If it starts on land, the swimmer has 20 seconds maximum before an entry to the water is made. In a team routine the timing of the landwork is ended as the last swimmer enters the water.

The entry should be very much an integral part of a routine and it is important that there is a smooth transition from landwork to waterwork. Whatever type of entry is chosen it is essential that it is well executed. A bad entry can completely ruin an otherwise good routine.

The method depends a great deal on the ability of the swimmers. Head-first (dive) entries are definitely more difficult but can look beautiful if well done. A well executed plain header dive can be a very effective transition from landwork to waterwork. Variations in dives can add interest. A twist within a dive looks good; pike or tuck dives are possibilities, and a back dive could be very dramatic. A head-first entry which starts off as a handstand on the poolside looks very effective, but demands a high level of gymnastic skill!

Feet-first entries are easier and they do allow for variations, for instance in arm or head positions, to add interest. The photographs show feet-first entries with asymmetric arm position and a turn of the head to the side. Body tension is vital. Swimmers can also add effect by turning in mid-air after take-off. The degree of turn can be varied too; it may just be a quarter turn or a complete 360-degrees.

The take-off for a feet-first entry can be a step or a jump from one foot or two feet. In a duet or a team routine it is essential to make sure that everyone does the same take-off. It only takes one swimmer to spoil the whole effect by doing something different!

Obviously, the more swimmers there are, for instance in teams, the greater the possibilities for unusual entries. At competitions that I have visited I have been delighted by some of the variations. It may be that all the swimmers enter together, or in a canon formation (ie one after the other in quick succession), an arrowhead formation, pairs formation, or half the team first then the rest. Often teams use a combination of feet-first and head-first entries. Linkage of swimmers on the deck just prior to entry can also create a pleasing pattern.

The most unusual entry I ever saw was in a team routine where eight swimmers, instead of doing landwork and entry, got into the water in a line and, holding the trough, took up an inverted vertical position. They used their legs to gesture while still holding the trough and then their 'entry' consisted of letting go of the side and travelling inverted, still using leg gestures. Most effective, but obviously not for the beginner!

The 'follow on' phase, once the swimmers have entered the water, should continue the smooth transition from landwork to waterwork. Some thought should be given to the length of time spent under water, and there is quite a lot of concern at present about the physiological effects on a swimmer who

Asymmetric, feet-first entry   Feet-first entry from a sitting position

remains submerged for too long. However, the main thing is that after entry the swimmers need to get away from the poolside.

It is surprising how many swimmers think that they cannot be seen underwater. But the underwater phase after entry is very much a part of the routine. In duets and teams, it is essential that all swimmers do the same during this initial phase, whether travelling on the front or back, feet first or head first, or performing a figure. It is definitely not a chance to adjust costume or noseclip or simply relax.

The next stage to consider is how the swimmers will surface. They can come up head first, perhaps with arms leading either into a gesture or strokes, or just by sculling into a back or front layout. Feet first surfacing is another possibility, either by arching out into a back layout using the torpedo scull or coming up in an inverted vertical and performing part of a figure or hybrid. A flamingo or a single or double ballet-leg position could also be adopted. It is an opportunity for swimmers and teachers to use their imagination.

The whole area of entry and follow-on is often left very much to chance which is a great pity, because it can do so much to enhance a routine and help to hold it together.

DUET ROUTINE

Music: 'Lisa the Huntsman's Lass' and 'Lichtenstein Polka' from 'Polka Party' by James Last, Polydor 2371 190.

Beats of music	*Action*
1–8	Landwork.
1–2	Travelling towards shallow end using egg-beater kick (side by side). Swish right arm 90 degrees to the side and close, twice. Head follows arm.
3–4	2 breaststrokes.
5–6	Swish left arm 90 degrees to the side and close, twice. Head follows arm.
7–8	2 breaststrokes.
1–4	Facing shallow end, get into front pike.
5–8	Sit, back parallel to pool bottom, heels at surface.
1–4	Surface and quarter turn anti-clockwise into tub position. (Swimmers now one in front of the other.)
5–7	Travel head first in tub position.
8	Quarter turn in tub position so that feet are facing the deep end. (Swimmers now side by side.)
1–4	Straighten knees out and travel one behind the other using standard scull towards the shallow end.
5–6	Lift right leg 6in and lower. Head looks to the right.
7–8	Lift left leg 6in and lower. Head looks to the left.
1–3	Prepare for dolphin circle. Linked feet to head, travel head-first along surface towards shallow end.
4	First swimmer submerges.
5–11	Travel round dolphin circle (beats counted for first swimmer).
12	First swimmer surfaces.
13–16	Travel along surface.
1–2	Get into tub position.
3–4	Lift right leg into half-flamingo position.
5–8	Turn 180 degrees to face shallow end. (First swimmer turns clockwise, second swimmer turns anti-clockwise.)
1–2	Get into tub position.
3–4	Lift left leg into half-flamingo position.
5–8	Turn 180 degrees to face deep end. (First swimmer turns clockwise, second swimmer turns anti-clockwise.)
1–2	Come up to vertical, arms bent in front. (Right shoulder faces diagonally forwards to deep end, left shoulder faces diagonally backwards to shallow end.)

Beats of music	Action
3–4	Swish to the right, both arms opened out to sides, diagonally forwards, head following right arm.
5–7	Lift left arm up to 65 degrees, palm in; bend so that back of hand faces cheek, and straighten again (1 beat for each movement). Travel is forwards on the right diagonal, swimmers side by side.
8	Swing both arms round 180 degrees to face along opposite diagonal.
1–4	Canoe travel forwards on left diagonal towards shallow end, swimmers side by side.
5–6	Roll onto back (towards left shoulder).
7–8	Flat scull on the spot.
1–3	Bend right knee (thigh at 90 degrees).
4	Lift right leg into single ballet-leg position.
5–7	Right leg crosses over to water surface (as for Eiffel Tower).
8	Swish right leg across surface to meet left leg and roll to front.
1–2	Roll onto back (towards left shoulder).
3–6	Travel head first towards shallow end (standard scull). Swimmers side by side.
7–8	Oyster.
1–7	Travel under water.
8	Surface, side by side, right shoulder to shallow end.
1–8	4 back crawl strokes with swishing arm action (2 beats per stroke). Travel across pool, right shoulder to shallow end. Side by side.
1–6	Turn to left, travel towards deep end, one in front of the other using 3 straight-arm front-crawl strokes (2 beats per stroke). (Arm lift and recovery take 1 beat each, head follows lifting arm.)
7–8	Get into tub position, right shoulder to deep end, side by side.
1–2	Quarter turn in tub position so that feet face deep end.
3–4	Quarter turn.
5–6	Quarter turn.
7–8	Quarter turn.
1–4	Tuck up and execute somersault back tuck.
1	Straighten right leg.
2	Straighten left leg.
3	Bend and stretch right leg. Look right.
4	Bend and stretch left leg. Look left.
5–8	Kick, travelling head first, side by side.
1–4	Tuck both legs through to front layout.

Beats of music	Action
5–8	Execute somersault front tuck.
1–4	Tuck legs through and execute quarter turn so that feet are towards deep end. (Side by side.)
5–8	Torpedo scull.
1–4	Marlin, quarter turn, right shoulder to shallow end.
5–8	Marlin, quarter turn, feet to shallow end.
1–2	Lift right arm and lower.
3–4	Breaststroke, side by side.
5–6	Lift left arm and lower.
7–8	Breaststroke.
1	Swish left arm 90 degrees to left.
2	Swish right arm to join left.
3–4	Breaststroke.
5–8	Repeat left and right arm swishes and breaststroke. (Now travelling side by side to deep end.)
1–2	Get into front pike.
3–4	Sit.
5–6	Rotate 180 degrees (feet to shallow end).
7–8	Lower left leg.
1–4	Surface in back layout, feet to shallow end, side by side.
5–6	Straight-arm back crawl, right arm leading.
7–8	Straight-arm back crawl, left arm leading.
1–4	Single ballet leg with right leg, travelling towards deep end. (1 beat for each phase as leg lifts and lowers.)
5–8	Single ballet leg with left leg, still travelling towards deep end.
1–2	Bend and straighten both legs. Look right.
3–4	Bend and straighten both legs. Look left.
1	Come up to vertical and swish arms open.
2	Lift right arm 45 degrees and look at hand.
3	Bend right arm keeping elbow high.
4	Swish both arms through to front. Palms down.

TEAM ROUTINE (8 swimmers)

Music: 'Music Box Dancer', Frank Mills. Cassette: 'Music Box Dancer' (EMI EJ260284).

NB: Pool pattern continues as shown until a new diagram is given.

Beats of music	Action	Pool pattern (NB: deep end to top)
	Start in two rows across the pool, at shallow end.	
1–2	First row: from back layout standard scull towards deep end.	
3–4	Second row: from back layout standard scull towards deep end.	
1–4	First row: somersault back tuck.	
5–8	Second row: somersault back tuck.	
1–8	All swim 8 bent-arm back crawl strokes towards deep end. Roll onto front on 8th beat.	
1–8	All swim 8 bent-arm front crawl strokes towards deep end. Roll onto back on 8th beat.	
1–4	Slowly get into the tub position.	
1–2	Rotate 90 degrees clockwise in tub position.	
3–4	Rotate 90 degrees clockwise in tub position.	
5–6	Rotate 90 degrees clockwise in tub position.	

Beats of music	Action	Pool pattern (NB: deep end to top)
7–8	Rotate 90 degrees clockwise in tub position, and on eighth beat roll over into front layout.	
1–8	Swim 8 breaststrokes towards deep end as follows: normal breaststroke (1); swish and look to right (2); normal breaststroke (3); swish and look to left (4); repeat last 4 actions (5–8). (Roll onto back on eighth beat.)	
1–4	Standard scull towards deep end.	
1–8	Execute 4 marlin quarter turns. (Each turn takes 2 beats.)	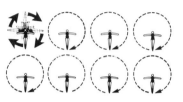
1–4	Standard scull towards deep end.	
1–4	Reverse scull towards shallow end.	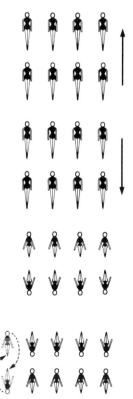
1–2	All get into tub position and second row turn clockwise to face partner feet-to-feet.	
3–5	Reverse scull in tub position until back-to-back with partner.	

Beats of music	Action	Pool pattern (NB: deep end to top)

Pool pattern
(NB: deep end to top)

6–8   Standard scull to return to starting position, feet-to-feet.

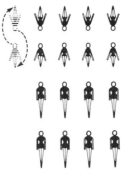

1–2   Second row: turn feet to shallow end. All show a back layout.

3–4   All submerge in oyster.

5–8   Surface from oyster in circle formation.

1–8   Reverse scull in circle formation clockwise.

1–2   Turn feet towards circle centre.

3–6   Kick gently and hold circle formation.

TEAM ROUTINE (8 swimmers)

Music: 'This is My Song', James Last. Cassette: 'Love. This is my Song' (Polydor 3150235).

Beats of music	Action	Pool pattern (NB: deep end to top)
	Start in two rows across the pool, near shallow end.	
1–8	Introduction and preparation.	
1–8	All breaststroke towards deep end. Roll onto back on eighth beat.	
1–8	Bent-arm back crawl towards deep end.	
1–8	Reverse scull towards shallow end.	
1–8 Crescendo in music	Standard scull towards deep end. Rotate onto front.	
1–8	Canoe travel towards shallow end.	

84

Beats of music	Action	Pool pattern (NB: deep end to top)
1–8	Travel into circle and assume back layout with feet facing centre, but not closed into centre.	
1–4	In tub position, 4 quarter turns (clockwise).	
5–8	In tub position, 4 quarter turns (anti-clockwise).	
1–6	Move in towards centre of circle with reverse scull.	
7–8	Submerge in oyster.	
1–4	Rise to surface.	
5–6	Lift arms up and open out.	

85

GROUP ROUTINE (20 swimmers)
Music: 'The Thorn Birds Theme' James Galway and Henry Mancini.
Cassette: 'In the Pink' (RCA RK 853125).

Beats of music	Action	Pool pattern (NB: deep end to top)
	Group A start with feet to deep end. Group B start with feet to shallow end. Begin towards deep end.	
1–4	Flat scull, preparation.	
1–8	Reverse scull if in Group A. Standard scull if in Group B. Both groups travel to deep end.	
1–2	On the spot, bend right knee and straighten.	
3–4	On the spot, bend left knee and straighten.	
1–8	Reverse scull if in Group B. Standard scull if in Group A. Both groups travel to shallow end.	
1–2	All assume tub position.	
3–4	Group A (feet to deep end) turn 90 degrees clockwise. Group B (feet to shallow end) remain stationary.	
5–6	Group A rotate 90 degrees clockwise in tub position.	
7–8	All lift and lower right leg so that ankle/heel finishes at the surface (leg straight). Then repeat with left leg (1 beat per leg).	

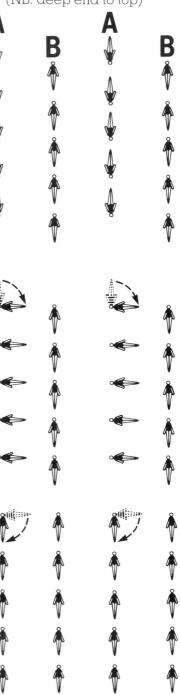

Beats of music	Action	Pool pattern (NB: deep end to top)

1–2	All rotate 90 degrees clockwise in tub position.
3–4	Lift and lower right leg. Then repeat with left leg (1 beat per leg).

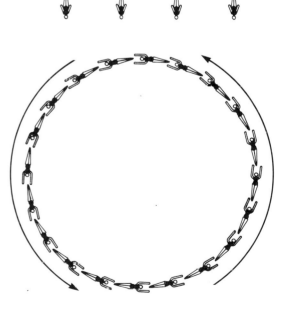

5–6	All rotate 90 degrees clockwise in tub position so all feet are to deep end.
7	Stretch into back layout.
8	Roll onto front, right shoulder leading.
1–8	Canoe travel towards shallow end.

1–8	Swim 8 breaststrokes into circle anticlockwise.

1–2	Tuck legs through to back layout.
3–6	Standard scull, maintaining circle.
7–8	Flat scull on the spot.

87

Beats of music	Action	Pool pattern (NB: deep end to top)

1–4   Maintaining back layout, rotate inwards so that feet face centre of circle.

5–8   Reverse scull in towards centre, closing into tub position to make the circle smaller.

1–4   Open out into back layout and standard scull outwards.

5–8   Travel gently, kicking legs, maintaining circle.

DISPLAYS

Displays are rewarding but exhausting to produce, demanding creativity, innovation, imagination, loads of hard work, unending patience and a great sense of humour. They can be produced for open days, festivals or commemoration days. There is tremendous flexibility and really no limit to the number of people who can take part. I have swum in display routines with as many as forty swimmers. Displays can follow a definite story or can be based on a particular theme. Water pantomimes are very popular ie Cinderella, Jack and the Beanstalk, Snow White etc.

The simplest display could just contain a variety of solo, duet and team routines, but it is possible to use a mixture of land and water work, and the two can be combined very successfully. One Christmas I took part in an 'Aqua Spectacular' which included solo, duet and team routines, diving, canoeing, rhythmic gymnastics, dance, a choral group and a school band. The grand finale of the show was eight swimmers, with 'antler' head-dresses and reins, pulling through the water a floating sleigh containing Father Christmas. A real masterpiece!

Such shows are tremendous entertainment for participants and spectators alike, but good organisation is vital if everything is to run according to plan. The following points need to be considered carefully:

1 The order of the programme must be arranged so that one act leads smoothly into another.
2 Scene changes should take as little time as possible so that long breaks in action are avoided.
3 Lighting must be positioned to give emphasis to specific performers or areas and possibly to create special effects.
4 Costume should be colourful and pleasing to the audience
5 Suitable props must be chosen for use on land or in the water.

Participants can rehearse either individually or as groups but plenty of time must be allowed for full rehearsals so that the whole display is co-ordinated.

COMPETITIONS

All competitions are made up of two parts: (a) figures; (b) routines.

Every competitor performs the figures, which are drawn up by the referee before the competition commences. Entry to the solo, and team duet routine competition is usually by qualification from the figure section. For example, the swimmers with the top ten figure scores might qualify for the solo competition and the swimmers with the ten highest combined figure scores might qualify to swim their duets. The number of swimmers who qualify for the solo and duet routines would really depend on the overall number of entries to the competition.

Each club competing may enter a team, which should be between four and eight swimmers. It is an advantage to have more than four because for each additional swimmer a ½-mark bonus is awarded, even before the team enters the water: ie five swimmers = ½-mark bonus; six = 1-mark bonus; seven = 1½-mark bonus; eight = 2-mark bonus.

Marking
Figures are usually marked by a panel of five or seven judges. Marks are awarded as follows:

½–2½ Unsatisfactory.
3–4½ Deficient.
5–5½ Satisfactory.
7–8½ Good.
9–10 Very good.

When the marks for a figure are shown, the scorers discard the highest and the lowest mark and divide the remaining three or five marks by the remaining three or five judges, to give a mean score.

Scores for routines are given in tenths instead of in halves. The highest and lowest marks are discarded and the result is multiplied by ten and then divided by the total number of judges, less two.

Costumes
Costumes for the figure competition must be plain and dark and worn with a plain white cap. Costumes for the routine competition must be one-piece and devoid of openwork.

Pool Dimensions
The pool must have an area of at least 12m (40ft). The depth for the figure competition must be at least 3m (10ft), and for routines 1.7m (6ft).

Timing
A solo swimmer is allowed 3.30 minutes, plus or minus 15 seconds; duets have 4 minutes, plus or minus 15 seconds; teams have 5 minutes, plus or minus 15 seconds. These times are inclusive of 20 seconds allowed for deckwork. The timing of a routine starts and ends with the accompaniment.

Officials
In addition to the judges the following officials are required to be in attendance at a competition: a referee; an assistant referee; clerks of the course; scorers (two per panel of judges); timers (two); a music controller; general helpers (as many as possible); an announcer.

6 Lesson Plans

SCHOOL TIMETABLE

Synchronised swimming can be used as a contrasting activity for part of a school swimming lesson or as a complete lesson on its own. Below are listed some of the skills which may be introduced to the curriculum at primary, middle and upper level.

Primary

1 Basic sculls: standard; reverse; flat.
2 Basic figures: tub; oyster; somersault back tuck; log roll; marlin.
3 Changing from one scull to another smoothly, perhaps accompanied by a drum beat or music, and linking sculls with simple stunts to form sequences also provide a challenge. The children can work alone, in pairs or small groups.

Middle

1 Sculls: standard; reverse; flat; canoe travel; plus possibly dolphin and torpedo, depending on the ability of the class
2 Strokes: back crawl, plus variations.
3 Basic figures: tub; oyster; somersault back tuck; log roll; marlin; somersault front tuck.
4 The teacher can provide accompaniment for stroke work, initially by using a drum or tambour, progressing to using music. Sculling, strokes and figures can be linked together to form sequences. Children should experience working in pairs and groups.

Upper

1 Strokes: back crawl; breaststroke; front crawl; plus variations, with the use of a drum beat and music as accompaniment. The children can practise swimming in ranks and keeping in line with others.
2 Sculls: standard; reverse; flat; canoe travel; dolphin; torpedo; and an introduction to the support scull.
3 Figures: tub; oyster; somersault back tuck; log roll; marlin; somersault front tuck; somersault front pike. Also, depending on ability, possibly: single ballet leg; somersub; dolphin; kip.
4 The eggbeater kick can also be introduced, as can head-first and feet-first

entries. Strokes can be swum in ranks to music and different swimming formations can be experimented with. Sequences to music can be created combining sculls, strokes and figures, and these can be performed in pairs or in groups of various sizes.

CLUB TIMETABLE
Proficiency in all four normal swimming strokes is desirable and time should be spent on this. General swimming training should be used as a warm-up to each session but should also be used on its own to improve strength and endurance. The following skills can be introduced, according to the ability of the group:
1 Sculls: standard; reverse; flat; canoe travel; dolphin; torpedo; lobster; reverse lobster; for piking, the support, Russian and scoop sculls, and the reverse dog paddle; plus twists and spins, and the egg-beater kick.
2 Strokes: back crawl; breaststroke; front crawl; plus variations and different formations.

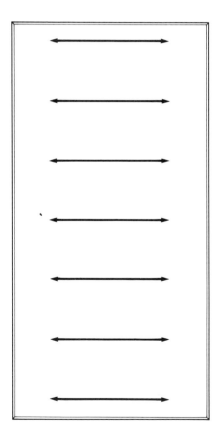

Plan 1 For pupils working widthways, individually or with a partner

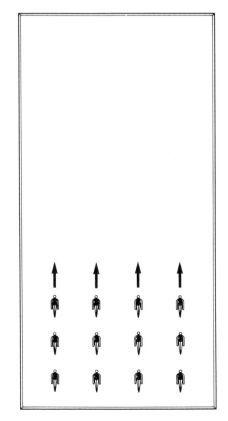

Plan 2 For pupils working lengthways in ranks – swimmers must keep in line

3 Figures: grades I-V in order of progression, as listed in the ASA Handbook of Synchronised Swimming.

4 Routines: solos and duets for the more advanced club members – either in preparation for grades IV or V or for competition; team routines, maybe for competition or display purposes.

5 In addition to the above activities, time should be given to landwork which may include weight-training, flexibility, gymnastics and dance. Routines may also be 'walked through' on land to check on timing and positioning.

POOL PLANS FOR STROKE AND SCULLING PRACTICE

The length, width and depth of the pool must be carefully considered. The teacher should experiment with various pool plans. Courlene rope is essential and can be tied or hooked to the rail. If there is no rail, brackets can be made to hook into the trough or edge of the bath surround. The rope can divide the pool lengthways and widthways. Suggested activities for stroke and sculling practice are given in Chapters 2 and 3.

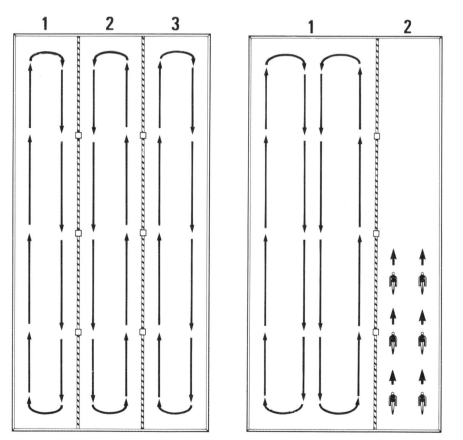

(left) *Plan 3* For chain swimming in roped-off lanes. Lanes 1 and 3 swim clockwise; lane 2 swims anti-clockwise. Swimmers should be a few yards apart. (right) *Plan 4* For chain swimming in roped off areas. Lane 1: stroke activities in two chains, one swimming clockwise, the other anti-clockwise. Lane 2: sculling in two ranks.

POOL PLANS FOR MIXED-ABILITY LESSONS

The pool can be divided into sections, using courlene rope if necessary, to allow different ability groups to work alongside each other. Two examples are given below:

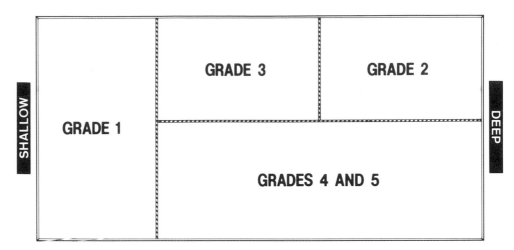

Plan 5
Grade 1: sculling widthways across the pool.
Grade 2: head-first and feet-first entries.
Grade 3: learning new figures.
Grades 4 and 5: swimming half lengths, working on single and double ballet legs and egg-beater kick.

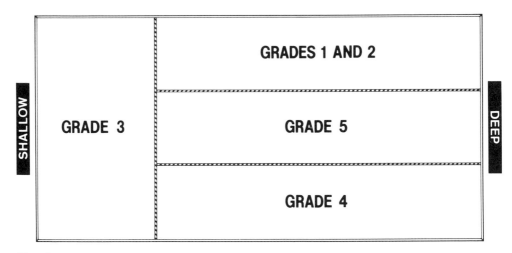

Plan 6
Grades 1 and 2: figures.
Grade 3: sculling.
Grade 4: non-routine swimmers working on figures in pairs.
Grade 5: routine.

With a single-ability group, all could work first on general strokes and then on sculling. If synchronised swimming strokes are being taught the pupils can swim in ranks, keeping in line as they go up the length.

LESSON PLAN 1

Time: 20 minutes   Number in class: 6   Equipment: tambour
Aim: to teach beginners the standard, reverse and flat sculls
(TP=teaching points)

Introduction

Breaststroke widthways.	**TP** Think about continuity and rhythm.

Main Theme

1 Standard scull.

(a) Teacher's explanation and demonstration.	**TP** Can you propel yourself head first using arms only? Elbows straight. Arms close to sides. Fingers upwards. Hands firm. Imagine you are wiping windows. Now can you push towards your feet as you wipe?
(b) All class try.	**TP** As (a).
(c) Check body position.	**TP** Keep feet up (scull harder if they sink). Head back. Tummy up.
(d) All try again.	**TP** Teacher finds pupil to demonstrate TPs.

2 Reverse scull.

(a) Teacher's explanation and demonstration.	**TP** Can you travel feet first using arms? Arms straight and close to sides. Fingertips point downwards. Hands firm. Fingers together. Think about body position. Use a tiny breaststroke pull, but use hands only. Now can you push the water towards your head and travel feet first?
(b) All class try.	**TP** Teacher finds pupil to demonstrate TPs.

3 Flat scull.

(a) Teacher's explanation and demonstration.	**TP** Can you stay on the spot using arms only? You need to push downwards. Think about all the points previously mentioned.
(b) All class try.	**TP** Teacher finds pupil to demonstrate TPs.

Conclusion

Start off head first, sculling to a drum beat. On the first heavy beat change to reverse scull and on the next heavy beat change to flat scull.

Contrasting Activity

Tub. (This figure uses the two sculls that the class have learnt.)	**TP** Start in a back layout, using flat scull to keep stationary. Increase speed of sculling to get into the tub position. To rotate: one hand does standard scull and the other hand does flat scull. Open out to a back layout again using flat scull.

LESSON PLAN 2

Time: 20 minutes   Number in class: 6   Equipment: tambour
Aim: to teach the class tub and oyster
(TP=teaching points)

Introduction

Bent-arm back crawl.	**TP** Concentrate on rhythm and low leg kick. Scull with free hand, keep head up to see and hear.

Main Theme

1 Tub.

(a) Flat back layout.	**TP** Use flat scull. Elbows straight, arms close to the sides, head back. Press down to keep the body up. Tummy and toes to the surface.
(b) Into tub position.	**TP** Flat scull harder and slowly draw the knees towards the chest. Keep the lower legs at the surface. Thighs should be at 90 degrees to the water surface.
(c) Turning in the tub position.	**TP** To rotate: use a standard scull with the right hand and a flat scull with the left hand. This will cause you to turn to the right. Rotate 360 degrees. As you rotate, keep your head back and imagine that you are sitting on a drawing pin!
(d) Opening out to back layout.	**TP** Use a flat scull to open out. Keep head back and lower legs at the water surface.
(e) Repeat whole figure.	**TP** As above. Can you synchronise with a partner?

2 Oyster.

(a) Back layout.	**TP** as 1a.
(b) Pike and sink.	**TP** Palms face down in flat scull position. Then sweep arms and hands outwards until they are level with the shoulders. Turn hands so that palms face upwards. Arms then push up over the head and, at the same time, the hips pike and legs push up. Hands should touch ankles in a closed-pike position. Sink.

Conclusion

Tub and oyster, synchronising with a partner.	**TP** As for 1 and 2.

Contrasting Activity

Sequence (working with a partner). Teacher accompanies on tambour.	**TP** Bent-arm back crawl, 4 strokes. Tub figure, then into oyster.

96

LESSON PLAN 3

Time: 20 minutes   Number in class: 6

Equipment: cassette player and music 'Commando General', by The Band of HM Royal Marines commando forces, from the cassette 'And the Band Played On', EMI TCEML 3434.

Aim: to work on the sculls needed to attain a front-pike position and then to use this within figures (TP=teaching points)

Introduction

(a) Working widthways, back-crawl leg kick.

TP Keep leg kick below surface, to regular beat. Hands on thighs. Head up, chin tucked in.

(b) Widthways, bent-arm back crawl (using music).

TP Keep leg kick going. Elbows high. Scull at hips with free hand. Keep in line with other swimmers.

Main Theme

1 Front-pike position.

(a) Teacher's explanation and demonstration.

TP Trunk at 90 degrees to legs. Three different sculls – Russian, reverse dog paddle and scoop – can be used to get into pike. Travel half a body length into it. Use of body is vital when pressing firmly into pike.

(b) From front layout use Russian scull to attain pike.

TP Good flat body in layout. Heels and hips at the surface. Flat scull to remain stationary. Hands then scull *slowly* to a position in advance of the head about a foot below the surface. Russian scull: firm hands, elbows slightly bent. Press up towards surface with 'meaty bit' of the hands, then tuck elbows into sides. Angle hands back so palms face bottom. Press down then scoop hands round to recommence. When in front-pike position scull behind hips with palms down to balance.

(c) Attaining front pike using reverse dog paddle or scoop. (Try both methods.)

TP Reverse dog paddle: keep elbows in and give mostly upwards pressure. (Some forwards pressure is inevitable.) You will need to use reverse lobster scull to initiate forwards movement before transferring hands through to do reverse dog paddle. Rotating scoop: keep elbows wide and imagine that you are moving your trunk through your hands. Pressure is mainly upwards.

Conclusion

Use the front-pike position in a figure.

TP As appropriate to chosen figure. Suggestions: somersault front pike; somersub; porpoise; catalina reverse.

LESSON PLAN 4

Time: 20 minutes   Number in class: 6
Equipment: cassette player and music, 'Bobby Crush Singalong Party',
Warwick WWA5138; also 'plastic man' or artist's lay figure.
Aim: to work on dolphin scull and then to use it in the early progressions of
walkover back (TP=teaching points)

Introduction (5 minutes)

(a) Swim widthways
using your favourite
normal stroke.

TP Think about the rhythm of the stroke.

(b) Dolphin scull.
(Working widthways.
Brief spoken introduction
given before starting.
One pupil chosen to
demonstrate if suitable.)

TP Keep body stretched and fully extended.
Elbows straight, arms shoulder width apart.
Hands firmly 'on the shelf', wrists raised. Equal
pressure towards feet on inward and outward
parts of the scull.

Main Theme (10 minutes)
Walkover back.

(a) Back layout,
transition into the arched
back position.

TP Flat body position, eyes look up, tummy and
feet up. Flat scull in advance of the head.
(Check that there is no jerking and no head or
feet first travel.) Hands smoothly into
dolphin-scull. Travel half a body length at the
surface before beginning the roll back. Dolphin
scull and 'roll over barrel' until head is in line
under the hips.

(b) Transition into split
position.

TP Push head right back as you lift the first leg.
Hands move from dolphin scull to either support
scull or flat scull behind the ears. In split
position the head must be in line and hands
support scull or flat scull behind the ears.
Push/press both legs down on the water surface
in split position and keep hips square.

(c) Complete back
walkover with emphasis
on the arch-back/split
transition.

TP As above.

Conclusion (5 minutes)
Synchronise strokes to
music, using back crawl
and front crawl. (Work in
pairs making up stroke
variations.)

TP As necessary. Check especially the leg
kicks – low down in the water and no splash.
Use the free hand to scull to keep body up and
balanced.

LESSON PLAN 5

Time: 20 minutes   Number in class: 6

Equipment: cassette player and music 'Commando General', by The Band of HM Royal Marines commando forces, from the cassette 'And the Band Played On', EMI TCEML 3434; also 'plastic man' or artist's lay figure.

Aim: to teach the twist (half and full) using mid-trunk support scull and then to incorporate it in certain figures (TP=teaching points)

Introduction (5 minutes)

(a) Swim widthways using bent-arm front crawl. (To music.)

TP Keep leg kick low. High elbow. Scull in front of body with free hand to help keep body up. Keep in line.

(b) Front crawl variations. (Work in pairs, choose own variations.)

TP As necessary.

Main Theme (10 minutes)

Twist (half and full).

(a) Support scull in inverted-vertical. (More advanced swimmers try this, and other practices in this lesson, in a crane or flamingo bent-knee position; alter path of sculling to avoid over-balancing or jerking.)

TP Keep scull as centralised as possible. Make sure that body position is firm, head in line, shoulders back, seat tucked in, legs stretched. Elbows about 4in from ribs. Imagine moving the backs of your hands over two molehills; when you push back the little finger lifts up and then slices; when you come forwards the thumb lifts and then slices. Palm pressure is towards the pool bottom.

(b) Decide which way you want to turn.

TP If you want to turn to the right your right hand angles on the forward part of the support-scull action. As you push forwards press your right shoulder back, maintaining a firm body position. Left hand flat sculls to keep body up.

(c) Try turning clockwise and anti-clockwise.

TP Remember that the hand on the side you are turning towards angles to help the turn, and the shoulder on that side pushes back.

(d) Try half and full twists. (More advanced swimmers aim for greater height.) Also try variations in leg positions.

TP As necessary.

Conclusion (5 minutes)

Half or full twists within a figure. (Pupil demonstrations can be used.)

TP As appropriate to chosen figure. Suggestions: porpoise, half twist; flamingo, full twist; catalina, full twist.

LESSON PLAN 6

Time: 20 minutes (it may not be possible to complete the whole sequence)

Number in class: 6

Equipment: cassette player and music 'Bunch of Thyme' by Brendan Shine, from 'My Old Country Home', Play LC1017; also 'plastic man' or artist's lay figure.

Aim: to teach the group a sculling sequence using formations

NB: Pool pattern continues as shown until a new diagram is given

Beats of music	Action	Pool pattern (NB: deep end to top)
1–4	(a) In two rows of three swimmers, standard scull towards deep end.	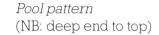
5–6	(b) Roll from back layout through 360° to back layout (anti-clockwise).	
7–8	(c) Flat scull on spot.	
1–4	(d) Reverse scull towards shallow end.	
1–2	(e) Into tub position.	
1–4	(f) Four quarter turns in tub position, clockwise. (One quarter turn on each beat.)	
1–8	(g) Canoe travel into circle. (From tub position swimmers 2, 3 and 6 tuck legs through to canoe position; swimmers 1, 4 and 5 stretch out in back layout and then roll to the left.)	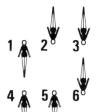 
1–4	(h) Tuck legs through to back layout.	
5–8	(i) Reverse/flat scull, moving into two lines of three.	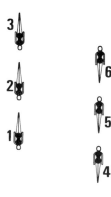

Beats of music	Action	Pool pattern (NB: deep end to top)
1–4	(j) Into tub position, quarter turn to the right to face partner.	
5–8	(k) Reverse scull hard and cross over left shoulders until head to head.	
1–4	(l) Stretch out to back layout and marlin quarter turn to the left.	
1–2	(m) Open and close legs (90 degrees).	
1–4	(n) Marlin, quarter turn to the right.	
1–2	(o) Pivot at surface so that feet are to deep end.	

Beats of music	Action	Pool pattern (NB: deep end to top)

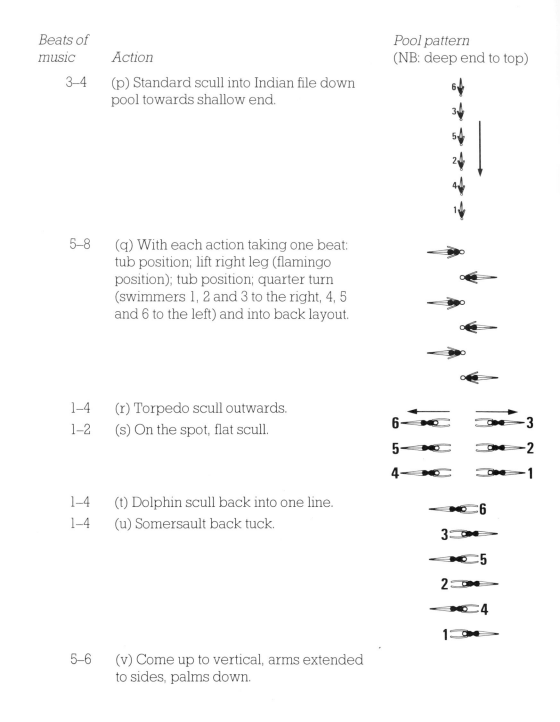

3–4   (p) Standard scull into Indian file down pool towards shallow end.

5–8   (q) With each action taking one beat: tub position; lift right leg (flamingo position); tub position; quarter turn (swimmers 1, 2 and 3 to the right, 4, 5 and 6 to the left) and into back layout.

1–4   (r) Torpedo scull outwards.

1–2   (s) On the spot, flat scull.

1–4   (t) Dolphin scull back into one line.

1–4   (u) Somersault back tuck.

5–6   (v) Come up to vertical, arms extended to sides, palms down.

7 Landwork, Fitness Training and Dance

Synchronised swimmers need to be fit. In addition to water skills, a landwork programme is essential to provide an all-round fitness programme. Landwork training must be carefully planned and requires a specialist teacher/coach to select the appropriate schedules for the swimmers. This chapter is a little technical but it is important for all swimmers who wish to reach their personal peak.

Dance and gymnastics also provide important experience, as many of the principles of dance and gymnastics can be applied in a synchronised swimming situation (see p112).

THE COMPONENTS OF FITNESS

An appropriate definition of the fitness required for synchronised swimming would be: the ability to carry out all the parts of any routine without too much strain and fatigue, leaving enough energy in reserve for a quick recovery in order that the routine may be repeated many times during a training session. This ability depends upon how well the following physiological components of fitness have been built up.

1 Flexibility   The ability to move a joint through a wide range of movement with as much ease as possible.
2 Strength   The ability to hold or move against heavy resistance.
3 Speed   The ability to move, either body parts or the total body, short distances in small intervals of time.
4 Power   The ability to move against resistance with speed. This component, defined as 'the rate of doing work', depends upon the development of *strength* and *speed*.
5 Endurance   This comprises:
(a) Muscular endurance – the ability to hold (static) or continue (dynamic) muscular contractions over periods of time.
(b) General endurance – the ability of the energy systems of the body to provide adequate energy supplies for muscular contractions to take place and to allow the body to recover quickly between each bout of work.

There are two energy systems within the body: *aerobic*, which enables oxygen to be utilised over prolonged and moderately intensive exercise;

and *anaerobic*, which enables the body to function when the intensity of the exercise cannot be met by the aerobic supplies.

Recovery for both systems is satisfied by the aerobic energy source.

The Principles of Training

Each component of fitness is optimally trained for by following certain principles:

1 **Specificity**   In simple terms, this means that the structure and content of the training programme must meet the requirements and demands of the sport involved.

2 **Adaptation**   The body will adapt to a programme of training and performance must then be improved by progression.

3 **Progression**   The improvement of performance is achieved through the principle of overload.

4 **Overload**   As the intensity of training is increased the body will adapt once more to a higher level of fitness.

5 **Generality**   The body is an aerobe that survives only in the presence of oxygen. Without oxygen the cells and tissues die. Therefore, whatever the fitness requirements of a task, aerobic endurance must be provided for somewhere within the training programme.

6 **Reversibility**   If the training stops the level of fitness deteriorates. Training may stop completely due to a lack of motivation, injury or out-of-season period, or a performer or coach may unknowingly neglect one component of fitness for the sake of others.

LANDWORK

This is a form of training whereby the swimmer can develop the components of fitness on land. Although it cannot be regarded as a substitute for water training, landwork can be useful in a number of ways:

(a) For warm-up exercises before a routine commences.
(b) To improve one or more of the components of fitness.
(c) To maintain the level of fitness when a pool is not available.
(d) To work through the choreography of a routine whilst under the close supervision of the coach.
(e) For warming-down after a routine is over, allowing maximum time in the water for more important work.

Landwork must be made enjoyable, varied and interesting, and must motivate the swimmer to carry over the effect into the water. Before deciding upon the content of a landwork training programme the coach must make a detailed analysis of the swimmer's routine and decide which components of fitness are specific to the demands made on the performer.

A brief analysis of a typical synchronised swimmer's routine reveals that:

(a) The majority of the routine is underwater and therefore most muscular contractions are made anaerobically.

(b) Sculling of the hands and kicking of the legs moves or holds the body in the water.

(c) The body extends, flexes, twists and turns into a wide variety of positions.

(d) Strong beating action of the legs brings the upper body out of the water as high as possible.

The greatest demands made upon the body are those which are satisfied by a high level of fitness in the components of: anaerobic endurance; dynamic and static muscular endurance; flexibility; power.

As a guideline to the coach the table below gives the value of each component marked out of 10 and the approximate percentage of training time that needs to be spent on it.

	Grade	% Time
Flexibility	10	30
Strength (see below)	2	1
Speed	5	3
Power	6	10
Static Muscular Endurance	5	4
Dynamic Muscular Endurance	10	25
Aerobic Endurance	3	2
Anaerobic Endurance	10	25

Strength can be defined as the maximal force that can be applied in a single contraction. A measure of dynamic strength is the maximal amount of resistance which can be moved in a desired direction. This is known as 'gross strength' and is trained for by *slowly* lifting maximal resistance for a small number of repetitions. Only in certain situations is this type of strength required by the synchronised swimmer, eg lifting the body weight from a straight leg position into a handstand on the side of the pool.

The strength requirements of the synchronised swimmer should be appropriate to the amount of resistance to be moved and this will be less than that used for gross strength gains. Therefore, the resistance used in landwork strength training should be of an intensity which relates closely to the amount of resistance and the specific way in which the body is moved in the water. The strength gains required by the swimmer will be developed by power and static/dynamic muscular endurance exercises. Nearly 40 per cent of the landwork training time should be devoted to the development of these components and this accounts for the relatively small percentage of time recommended for pure strength training in the table.

Specificity of training also refers to the body parts for which the component of fitness requires developing the most. Another important aspect is the pattern of movement which the body parts make in the water.

If the muscles are to be specifically trained for water work, then it is essential that an exact reproduction of the movement must be made on land.

Exercises

Landwork exercises can be divided into two categories: *general exercises*, which, although not specific, bring about improvement to the fitness components, eg squat thrusts for dynamic endurance; and *specific exercises*, which simulate the water fitness on land, eg sculling actions with weighted gloves.

In order that the swimmer is subjected to an anaerobic endurance effect all landwork exercises should be performed wearing a noseclip. Holding the breath for as long as possible will improve lung capacity and the ability of the swimmer to survive under the water whilst performing various skills.

Flexibility

This can be improved both generally and specifically by: neck rotation; shoulder rotation; hip and trunk rotation; wrist rotation; abduction-adduction of legs; ankles (see diagrams).

Dynamic and Static Muscular Endurance

Specific exercises can include:

(a) Holding a position at the extreme range of a flexibility exercise.

(b) Wearing weighted gloves and weighted shoes to provide resistance for sculling arm actions and beating leg actions. These actions performed over a period of time will improve dynamic muscular endurance.

Skipping exercises can bring about a general improvement in muscular endurance both in the arms and legs.

Power

General improvement in power can be brought about by activities such as lifting the body weight explosively in jumping, bounding, skipping and hopping.

Strength/Power

This will be improved generally by lifting activities, such as step-ups, press-ups and abdominal curls, where the speed is slower and more control over the body is necessary.

Power/Agility

Shuttle runs over varying distances improve this general component.

Circuit Training

This is an excellent form of landwork conditioning whereby both general and specific exercises can be combined, incorporating the development of all fitness components.

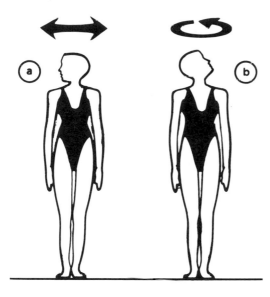

Flexibility exercises

(left) Neck rotation: a) look right then left, slowly; b) rotate head gently, in both directions

(centre left) Wrist rotation: hold both arms out in front and draw circles with the hands

(centre right) Abduction-adduction of legs: swing leg out to the side then across in front of body. Repeat with other leg

(bottom) Hip rotation: raise leg in front to horizontal, then swing to side horizontally and lower leg. Change legs and repeat

Flexibility exercises

(top) Trunk rotation: both arms swing up and back, bending trunk back gently, then swing arms round to front, bending gently forwards

(centre) Shoulder rotation: a) alternate arms work in a windmill fashion; b) both arms together press up and back, then return forwards

(left) Ankle rotation: sit with one leg out in front, cross other leg and, holding ankle, rotate foot. Change legs and repeat

WATERWORK

Fitness can be improved in the water by constant repetition of a routine or by taking a part of the routine which is weak and working the swimmer on that aspect. However, synchronised swimmers tend to neglect *general* fitness, often due to lack of water time. If general fitness training cannot be fitted into the synchronised swimming session, the swimmers should find time to work hard on their own and become proficient in the four normal strokes.

Stroke Counting

This is a useful method of analysing the performance of swimmers and helps to keep a check on stroke deterioration. The coach tells the pupils to count how many strokes they take for certain lengths, eg the third and sixth lengths they swim. The pupils count the number of times their arms complete a stroke cycle for each full length. (A stroke cycle is measured from commencement of the stroke's arm movement to its recommencement.) If the stroke count increases too much the swimmer may be slipping the water, ie during the underwater phase of the stroke there is a loss of purchase.

Bent arm back and front crawl, showing good high elbow position.

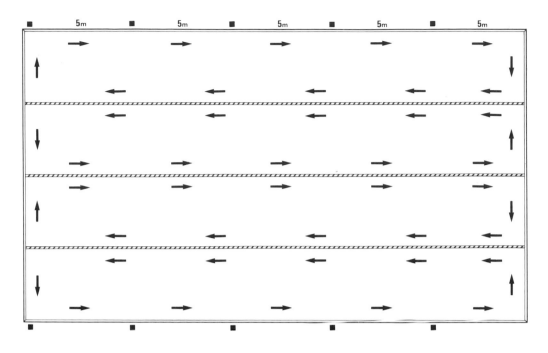

Time-control chain swimming

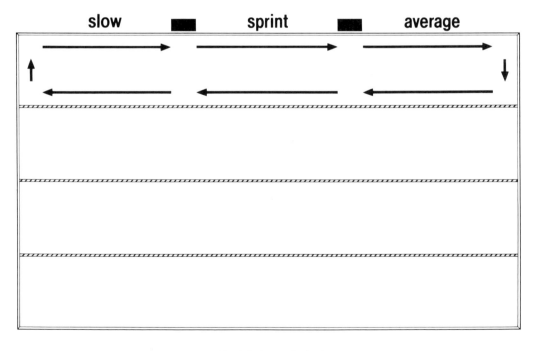

Fartlek (speed play)

Routines for General Fitness Training

1 Time control In this method chain swimming is used.
On each side of the pool, floats are placed at 5m intervals. Swimmers position themselves in the water in line with a float. On the start signal, they swim hard for a specified length of time, eg 30 or 60 seconds. At the end of the given time the distance covered by each swimmer is recorded. After an adequate rest period the exercise is repeated and the swimmers aim to improve on their distances.

2 Fartlek (speed play) This involves varying the pace of the swim. The length of the pool is divided into thirds and each third is swum at a different pace – slow, then sprint, followed by average pace. Swimmers work in lanes, chain swimming, for a set time, eg, 10 or 15 minutes.

3 Tempo/rest The coach sets a distance, eg, 50m, for the swimmer to swim, plus a number of times to repeat this distance, eg 10 × 50m. Between each 50m swim there is a period of rest which can be taken standing or swimming and can be used in different ways, as follows.
(a) Take the pulse before swimming and after every repetition. It will be about 60–80 beats to the minute at the start and may rise to upwards of 170 beats per minute after swimming. The fitter the swimmer, the faster the pulse rate will drop after each swim.
(b) The coach may specify the length of time for the swim and rest combined, eg, 10 × 50m, going every minute.
(c) The coach may specify the length of rest to be taken, eg, 10 × 50m, with 30 seconds rest.

4 Hungarian repetition This method offers variety and can include all strokes, with varied distances and necessary rest intervals. The sequence is

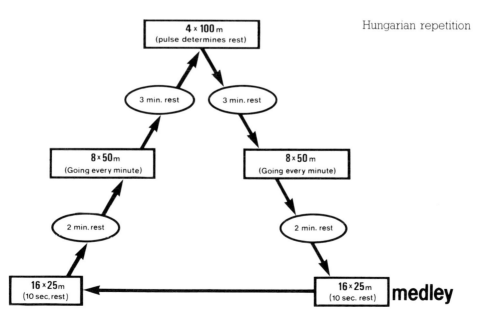

Hungarian repetition

111

shown in diagrammatic form as a triangle. Starting at the bottom left of the triangle, work through the repetitions on the left side, reaching the point of the triangle and working through the repetitions on the right-hand side. The repetitions can be swum as single strokes, medley, legs only, arms only, etc.

5 Broken swim   The swimmer is timed over a set distance from a push start, ie 100m (4 lengths of 25m), aiming to take 60 seconds. This is then broken down into lengths: ie 4 lengths in 60 seconds = 15 seconds/length. The swimmer is then allocated 10 seconds after each length for rest: 60 seconds swimming + 30 seconds rest = 90 seconds.

6 Full speed   This method of training is mainly for improving power. The swimmer covers the specified distance flat out and is then given a long rest period before repeating the exercise.

DANCE
Body Awareness
Body awareness is essential for synchronised swimmers, who must be encouraged to use the whole body by introducing ideas such as opening, closing, rising, falling, leaping and turning. As well as body awareness in movement, swimmers should be aware of what happens to the body when it is still. Still does not mean relaxed; as much muscular tension is needed to maintain stillness as is needed to move.

Within this area, experiment with symmetry and asymmetry in movement. It will soon be discovered that asymmetry creates a feeling of imbalance, and symmetry gives a sensation of balance: it is important to experience the contrast.

Concentrate on leading the movements with as many different body parts as possible – not just hands and feet. Try elbow, shoulder, hip or heel. This type of activity encourages an awareness of many more parts of the body in movement. Experiment also with weight transference and gesture; taking the body weight on parts other than the feet, for instance, then making movements with the feet and legs as would be done in water.

Spatial Awareness
Swimmers must be aware of the different *levels* that they can use: low, medium or high. Spatial dimensions are also important: up, down, right, left, forward and back. These dimensions, or combinations of two or three of them, can be used to create many interesting movements, and, when integrated with different levels, will give a much greater scope for expression – in, under and above the water.

These movements can be flexible or direct: a flexible movement uses the space to the full and indulges in it; a direct movement keeps to its path and does not deviate at all. Experiment with various types of movement within such 'pathways'.

Use of high level

Use of low level

Matching with a partner, using different levels

Symmetry at medium level

Asymmetry at medium level

Asymmetry in flight

Symmetry in flight

Forward roll in
gymnastic routine –
rounded shape

Cartwheel in gymnastic
routine – wide stretched
shape

Gymnastic exercises
Symmetrical balance

Asymmetrical balance ▼

Symmetrical balance with a partner ▶

Asymmetrical balance with a partner in gymnastic routine

Weight/Time Factors

The weight factors are firm and fine touch: a firm movement is 'strong', 'determined', 'with resistance'; a fine-touch movement is 'light', 'delicate', 'with little tension'.

The time factors are sudden and sustained: sudden movements are 'quick', 'sharp', 'instant', 'decisive'; while sustained movements are 'smooth', 'uninterrupted', 'lingering', 'gradual', 'unhurried'. Swimmers should experience these different factors in movements and should combine weight and time factors to vary mood and expression, eg, contrast a sudden firm movement with a sustained light-touch movement.

Flow

There are two types of flow: free and bound. In *Modern Educational Dance*, Laban describes free and bound flow as follows: 'In an action in which it is difficult to stop the movement suddenly, the flow is free. In an action capable of being stopped and held without difficulty, at any movement during the movement, the flow is bound.' Therefore we could say, that free flow is 'uncontrolled', 'with abandon', 'fluid', 'outgoing', and bound flow is 'restrained', 'cautious', 'controlled', 'limited'. Again, experiment with movements that contrast the two different types of flow.

Many of the factors discussed above can be applied to the synchronised swimming situation, especially in routines, and an experience of dance, however little, gives a useful advantage. Body awareness will help the swimmer to make full and greater use of the whole body. An awareness of space dimensions, levels and pathways can give endless variety of movement and pool pattern and creates interest. Use of weight and time factors can give contrasts in speed and tension in movement. In synchronised swimming movement is mainly in bound flow, but an appreciation of the difference between free and bound flow is useful.

GYMNASTICS

Gymnastics training can be very useful to the synchronised swimmer as it inevitably brings an improvement in general body management. Training can be in groups, pairs or individually, but should always be supervised by a qualified instructor. Apparatus can be used to increase scope and experience.

Encourage work in the following areas: transference of weight, travelling, flight, weight-bearing/balancing, on/off balance. In all of these areas, experiment with different types of movement, as follows.

a) Body tension – while moving or still.
b) Shape – flat, tucked, stretched, wide, twisted, rounded, narrow.
c) Direction – forward, backward, right, left, up, down.
d) Speed – fast, slow, still.
e) Size – large, small.

Acknowledgements

For their contributions to this book, our grateful thanks go to the following people: Joseph Dixon and Alan L. Williams (photography), Tony Butlin (fitness advisor) and Ethan A. Danielson (artwork).

We would also like to express our appreciation to the following associations, educational establishments and individuals for their contribution to our swimming experience.

The High School for Girls, Clifton, Bristol, England; The High School for Girls, Stroud, Glos, England; Coventry College of Education, England; Bedford College of Higher Education, England; The College of St Paul and St Mary, Cheltenham, England; The Physical Education Association of Great Britain and Northern Ireland; The Amateur Swimming Association, England; The Scottish Amateur Swimming Association; The Winston Churchill Memorial Trust, England; Mr Henry and Mrs Beulah Gundling, The International Academy of Aquatic Art, USA; Mrs Peg Seller, Canada; Miss Pauline McCullagh, Canada; Mr Don Kane, USA; Mrs Marian Kane, USA.

Thanks also to many other friends and colleagues in swimming too numerous to mention individually, and above all the hundreds of beginners and swimmers it has been our fortune to teach or coach.

Useful Addresses

The Physical Education Association
162 Kings Cross Road
London WC1X 9DH

The Institute of Swimming Teachers and Coaches
Lantern House
38 Leicester Road
Loughborough
Leics.

The Swimming Times
ASA (Amateur Swimming Association)
Harold Fern House
Derby Square
Loughborough
Leics.
LE11 0AL

The British Association of National Coaches
Oak Lodge
Theobalds Park Road
Enfield
Middlesex
EN2 9BN

Miss L V Cook
12 Kings Avenue
Woodford Green
Essex
IG8 0JB
(Synchronised swimming awards)

Index